# SEASONS
## *of the* SOUL

On Becoming Who You Are

MICHELLE DERUSHA

*In memory of Josie*
*My girl in all seasons.*

*For everything there is a season . . .*

ECCLESIASTES 3:1 ESV

# Contents

# An Invitation

I'm standing with my dog Josie at the curb, gazing up at the tree in my neighbor's front yard. I've passed this stately tree hundreds of times over several years of daily dog walks, and I've always marveled at how lush and green it is, no matter the time of year. On this particular September afternoon, though, I see something I've never noticed before. I see that the verdant leaves and vibrant orange berries I've long admired aren't actually part of the tree itself. Rather, they belong to an impressively large invasive vine that has wound its way up the tree's trunk and out along its limbs and branches.

What had looked like a beautiful, healthy tree is, in fact, an illusion. Not only is the vine obscuring the actual tree—an Austrian pine—that is languishing underneath, it is also clearly damaging the tree: blocking its sunlight, weighing it down, and slowly leeching it of nutrients. I see that beneath the thriving vine, the pine tree itself is dying, its needles crisped brown, its branches stiff and brittle.

From that day on, every time I pass the pine tree in my neighbor's yard, I stop for a few minutes to look up at it. As Josie impatiently tugs at the leash, I stare at the vine's thick stalks crisscrossing like a long plait all the way up the trunk. The vine has embedded itself into the tree's bark so seamlessly, I can hardly discern one from the other. I see that while the vine is flourishing—spreading its tendrils, reaching higher and higher, clutching and grasping—the pine tree itself seems thinner, weaker and more diminished every day.

Over time it becomes obvious to me: the tree is being swallowed by the vine.

*

This morning from my desk at the sunroom window I caught sight of the yellow iris waltzing in the spring breeze, ruffled petals swishing like the hem of a flamenco skirt. I don't typically cut iris to display in bouquets around the house, preferring instead to leave them standing in flamboyant clusters in the garden, where they remind me of a circle of gossiping ladies dressed in their Sunday best. Today, though, I had the sudden desire to place a single iris in a bud vase on my writing desk, and so, kitchen shears in hand, I walked barefoot out the back door, across the lawn and into the garden to choose one. Back inside, I slipped the tightly clasped bud into a glass of tepid water, set it next to my computer, and settled in to work, my feet still damp with morning dew.

Two hours later when I glanced up from my screen, I was surprised to see that one of the iris's lower petals had already begun to unfurl. After another two hours passed, the petal opposite the first had begun to open too, and by the end of the afternoon when I closed my laptop, the iris was in full bloom, petals splayed open to reveal its prickly beard curving like a colorful caterpillar from the stamen. The display looked like an invitation, and in the natural world, it is exactly that: a summons to bees and other insects to come close and dust their legs fuzzy with pollen before flying away to pollinate another flower.

The transformation of the iris from bud to bloom happened right before my eyes, and yet, I could not see it in progress. I witnessed the results—the petals wide open—but the process of getting from there to here was not discernible to me. This, it turns out, is often the way transformation works, not only in the natural world, but in our own selves and within our own souls as well. We don't always see or even feel our progression. We might wonder at times if anything is happening at all. And then one day we realize we have opened ourselves to receive the invitation.

Like the trees in our backyards and neighborhoods, and the iris in our gardens, we do not control the timing of our own transformation; there are forces larger than our individual selves at work here. But like the trees and flowers, we can open ourselves to the process, trusting that the Spirit is working in us, with us, and through us to prepare and create space for new life, even when we cannot yet see it.

I honestly never intended to write another book. As you'll read in the following pages, after releasing *True You*, my fourth book, in 2019, I stepped out of the publishing arena and away from my career as an author. I declared to myself, my agent, my editor, my family, my friends, and my readers that I was done writing books. And yet, here I sit at my writing desk at the sunroom window on a late spring day, writing another book.

The reason for this about-face is simple: I want you to know what I have learned over the past two years. Like the pine tree wrapped in the suffocating vine, I was once living a constricted and constrained life, a life in which I was not growing or flourishing, a life in which I was living small, stunted, and afraid. But I have learned there is another way. There is a "wide-open, spacious life" awaiting each one of us—a life God invites us to enter into (2 Corinthians 6:11–13). I want you to know this space and this freedom. I want you to live this wide-open, unconstrained, flourishing life.

When I stepped out of the publishing arena and quit book-writing, I assumed that part of my story had ended. I thought the last chapter had been written. Turns out, there are more chapters. My story doesn't end with quitting; quitting was just the beginning.

This is the story of a pine tree and a vine—the story of how I unwound the vine in order to uncover and begin to nourish my true self underneath. This is my story, but I believe your story is contained in these pages too. True, your vine is likely different than mine. You might not be wrapped up in achievement and vying for success like I have been. You might not be fixated on trying to earn your value and your worth through professional accomplishments like I was. But I suspect you have struggled (and perhaps still struggle) with a vine of your own—a way of being or thinking that has inhibited you from truly knowing, accepting, and loving yourself.

Most of us struggle to find our value in our own selves; instead, we look everywhere and at everyone else for our identity, for our definition of our worth. It is my hope that telling you this story of my vine will help you recognize your own vine and how or where it has wrapped its tendrils around you. It is my hope that this story of how I am learning to truly honor and love myself will help you do the same.

I've learned a lot about myself and about who God created me to be by observing nature and the cycle of the seasons over the last few years. I've learned there is much wisdom to be found in our own backyards and in the plants, animals, and insects with whom we share space. The natural world and the seasons teach us how to listen and see; they teach us what to hold on to and what to release, and how to allow ourselves to rest and to be replenished. Our natural surroundings can help us learn to recognize what depletes our soul and what sustains and enlivens us. The seasons and the natural world can teach us how to become more fully who God created us to be.

*Introduction*

Like the pine tree in my neighborhood, this self—the person God created and is always inviting us to become— has been there all along. It may be hidden, or buried or tangled up in habits or beliefs we don't need, but it is there. Let's unwind the vine. Let's uncover who is underneath. Let's say yes to God's invitation to become who we already are.

# PART 1

# Autumn
## *Release*

*Fulfillment demands that we let go.*
*We must fall into unknowing again, open*
*to an expectation without intention.*

GUNILLA NORRIS

# CHAPTER ONE

# Pine Tree and Vine

*Are you prepared to be other than your*
*image of your false self? If no, you will*
*live in bondage to your false self.*

RICHARD ROHR

My husband and I are sitting together on the living room sofa one February afternoon—me on one end, him on the other, the snow wisping against the windowpanes behind us—when he offers an observation that stops me cold. "The way I see it," Brad says gently, looking me in the eye, "your work as an author has brought you far more sorrow than joy."

I had been crying as we talked, the tears coursing down my face and neck, absorbing into the thick cotton neckline of my sweater. My book *True You* had been released a month prior, and I was expressing my disappointment and frustration over the outcome for what felt like the umpteenth time. *Why is my book not selling?* I lamented. *What did I do wrong? Why didn't so-and-so mention it? Why am I so bad at this?* And that's when Brad uttered the sentence that changed everything.

*True You* is about pruning away the extraneous, false parts of ourselves in order to live more authentically as the person God created us to be. I assumed when I finished writing it that I had reached the end of the journey toward uncovering my true self. I thought I'd "arrived." I patted myself on the back and congratulated myself on being "transformed" and "made new." And it wasn't untrue. Over the twelve months it took to write that book, God had shown me a lot about myself and invited me closer to him. I had indeed done some of the hard work of pruning and had uncovered parts of myself that had previously been unknown to me. As it turned out, though, there was much more pruning to be done and much more to be uncovered. Writing and releasing that book was only the very beginning of my journey toward letting go.

Leading up to and immediately following the publication of *True You* in January of 2019, I found myself in an extraordinarily fragile state. When I page through my journal entries from those months, I see the words "fragmented" and "disintegrated" scrawled in black ink again and again across the pages. I was coming apart, fraying at my physical, emotional, and spiritual seams. I couldn't concentrate. I felt agitated, restless, distracted and irritable. I had a pit of dread in the bottom of my stomach nearly all the time, but I didn't know why; I couldn't identify what I was dreading. I suffered from near-daily headaches; my jaw was making a disturbing clicking sound when I moved it side to side; I had a permanent knot just under my right shoulder.

Part of my mental and physical distress was simply the result of exhaustion. In the push to promote and release a book—my fourth in four years—in the middle of an already-hectic holiday season, I'd overextended myself. Shopping, gift wrapping, holiday gatherings, Christmas cards, traveling, baking, and decorating can send me off the rails in an ordinary season. Combining all that with working a part-time job, managing a book launch team, orchestrating social media promotions, writing extra articles and blog posts, and doing radio and podcast interviews obliterated whatever residual energy remained and catapulted me into a constant state of overwhelm.

Even worse than the physical and mental demands, though, was the emotional toll of the book release. The first few days of seemingly robust sales turned out to be the proverbial flash in the pan, and as interest fizzled and sales floundered, I grew more and more obsessed over why the book was not selling well. I checked its Amazon rank daily, on some days hourly. I constantly refreshed the page to see if the number of reviews posted were increasing and then despaired when I saw they weren't. I scoured Instagram and Facebook looking for mentions and shares about the book and was crushed when I realized it had barely made a ripple on social media.

It was clear from these benchmarks that the book's launch into the world was not going well. I also felt deeply hurt by the fact that many of the "influencers" I'd hoped would notice the book, particularly those who were authors themselves, hadn't mentioned it in their social media feeds, and I couldn't stop mentally harping over why.

*Do they not like the book?* I wondered. *Is the writing bad? Is the topic lame?* Or worse: *Do they just not like me?* I didn't consider that maybe many of those I'd hoped would champion my book simply had less bandwidth during the holiday season. I assumed it was all about me. I felt like I had failed, and I was devastated by and ashamed of my failure.

Brad's quiet declaration that February afternoon as we sat together on the living room sofa did not shock me. When I heard his words, I did not feel angry, hurt, or defensive. What I felt in that moment was relief—the kind of relief you experience in your whole body when a great burden has been lifted; the kind of relief you feel in your shoulders, in your jaw, in the very bottom of your gut.

I was relieved to hear spoken aloud what I had known deep down for many months, perhaps even for years. Brad said the words I was too afraid to say or even think myself.

But the moment I heard his words spoken aloud, I knew in my heart, mind, and soul that they were the absolute truth.

We have two choices when we recognize the truth. We can turn away and deny it—sweep it under the rug, pretend we didn't hear it or feel its seismic wave roll through our body. Or we can look it straight on and acknowledge it for what it is. In that moment on the sofa in the middle of a February snowstorm, I finally admitted what I knew was the truth. I nodded, agreeing, unable to speak through my closed throat, tears coursing down my cheeks. My work as an author—the work I considered to be my professional and personal calling, the work I'd thought I'd do for the rest of my life—had brought me far more sorrow than joy.

## Winding Experiences around Ourselves

In *The Gift of Being Yourself*, David Benner describes our calling as "the way of being that is both best for us and best for the world."[1] It turns out, my work as an author was not the calling I'd thought it was or had yearned for it to be, because it was not the way of being that was best for me. My husband saw the truth of that long before I did. I'm sure my children did too, though they didn't state it explicitly. But it took me much longer, in part because I so deeply and desperately desired book-writing to be my lifelong vocation.

To be clear, I don't believe the publishing industry is "bad." But I do believe that working in that professional space was bad for me because, as Paul put it in his first letter to the Corinthians, it reduced me to less than my true, God-created self (10:19–22). I was not living as my best self when I was working as an author. I was a diminished version of the person God created me to be, and because of that, I was also selling the world—and, more importantly, the people closest to me—short.

The afternoon Brad made his declaration from the sofa, I finally acknowledged that the culture of publishing was not a place in which I thrived as my best self. I finally admitted that I couldn't separate my self-identity from what felt like a relentless hustle to attract and attain more readers, more social media followers, and more blog subscribers. I couldn't separate my self from the Amazon ranks and the sales reports. I couldn't separate my self from the fact that, though I tried not to, I constantly compared myself to other authors. I couldn't rid myself of the jealousy that gripped my insides when I felt like I didn't measure up and from the bitterness that sat like a stone in my gut when I felt like I didn't fit in.

Nor, I realized, could I separate my self from the desire to be known, affirmed, and recognized by who I considered to be the "right" people—the influencers, the authors with the big social media platforms and legions of followers. I wanted to be part of the "in crowd." I wanted to be popular. I wanted to be bigger, better, and more. I wanted so badly to belong in that space and with those people—people I admired and whom I very much wanted to like me and admire me back. I pushed hard to be part of that space and a member of that group I esteemed so much. I pushed hard to belong.

I need to tell you, there's a story here that predates my work as an author. As with most things of any import, there are roots that go deep. Long before I ever wrote the first sentence of my first book, someone I knew once suggested that my job at the time was not good enough. I was working part-time as a writer in the fundraising department of the local PBS/NPR affiliate. It was a job I enjoyed and found fulfilling and challenging. Until, that is, I began to believe—based on someone else's opinion, which was undoubtedly formed by their own baggage and insecurities—that my work wasn't creative, interesting, or important enough. This person told me that although I had talent as a writer, I was wasting that talent in the work I was doing. I could do better, this person insisted.

I'm ashamed to say I believed this person. Wooed by their suggestion that I could become someone more, someone bigger, better and more valuable, and wanting to prove myself, I set my sights on writing a book. From the start, book-writing for me was linked to the hope and expectation that it could give me worth, make me special, and help me win others' approval and acceptance. Threaded through my entire ten-year publishing career was the hope that if I could do it right and be successful at it, being a published author would make me enough. I wrote to earn admiration. I wrote to earn my value and a place of belonging in the world. These were certainly not the only reasons I wrote four books, but these reasons were absolutely a driving force behind my ambition.

By the time the person who had originally devalued my work was no longer part of my life, the connection between writing and worth was firmly cemented in place. I simply turned my energy to earning the attention and approval of other authors I respected and admired—particularly those I considered to be in the inner circle of Christian publishing. I wanted to be noticed and seen by them; I wanted to be known and respected by them. I wanted to be valued by them and to have an esteemed place in their world.

In short, I made an idol out of being a "successful author," and as I funneled more and more of my energy toward sustaining my idol, I starved the other parts of my life. That February afternoon as I sat with my husband, I finally understood in the deepest part of me that my true, God-created self was like the pine tree in my neighbor's yard, and who I had become in my work as an author was the invasive vine I couldn't unwind.

I'd starved the pine tree to feed the voracious vine until I hardly recognized what was left of myself. And what I found beneath the façade of the vine, I didn't much like. I was bitter and jaded, petty, cynical, catty and jealous. I felt a deep sense of shame and failure. I was distracted and irritable. I complained relentlessly about my work. And I was exhausted—flat-out bone-weary from years of pushing to be more, do more, and become more. Supporting and maintaining the vine took a lot of energy. But underneath the illusion of green, healthy, vibrant leaves, I was a brittle, depleted husk.

"I use up my life in the desire for pleasures and the thirst for experiences, for power, honor, knowledge and love, to clothe this false self and construct its nothingness into something objectively real," Thomas Merton wrote in *Seeds of Contemplation.* "And I wind experiences around myself and cover myself with pleasures and glory like bandages in order to make myself perceptible to myself and to the world, as if I were an invisible body that could only become visible when something visible covered its surface."[2] Being a published author was a way for me to slake my thirst for power, honor, belonging, and love. My work was my way of winding experiences around myself, to build myself up and create stature and personhood for myself so that I would feel seen, known, and valuable.

The truth is, I liked the status my work as an author automatically earned me. When acquaintances asked what I did for a living, I felt proud to say I was a writer. Their reactions—an approving nod; an affirming, enthusiastic comment; their curiosity about what I wrote—reinforced my belief that my chosen profession impressed people, and I liked being impressive. I liked that when my boss at my part-time job introduced me to people, he always mentioned I was "a published author" with books in Barnes & Noble and on Amazon. He added those details every time, like it was a feather in his cap. In fact, he often talked more about the books I'd published than the work I did for him and the organization that employed us. As a result, I couldn't help but wonder: *Who would I be without the title of "published author"? Who would I be without that identity?*

I had wound the identity of being an author around and around myself until, in time, that identity became a substitute for my actual self. It was a false self, to be sure, but I couldn't see that. In the same way I mistook the vine for the actual tree all those times I had stood at the curb with Josie, I began to mistake my experiences, status, and identity as an author for my true self. In the end, rather than sustaining me and supporting me, my job—with its ego-inflating enticements of fame, glory, power, and belonging—held me hostage, ensnaring me and ultimately leeching me of contentment, joy, and life itself.

## Sacrifice, Surrender, Death

Every summer I spend a fair amount of my time in the garden pulling out vines that have invaded the flower beds, winding their tendrils up fence pickets and stems and around leaves and blooms. If you've ever tried to wrench a plant free from a strangling vine, you know how difficult it can be. It's meticulous, labor-intensive work, and I've learned that if I don't want to leave a bunch of mangled buds and blooms in my wake, I can't simply yank off the vines and be done with it. Instead, I methodically unwind each strand round and round down the flower's stem until I reach the spot with my fingertips where the vine is rooted in the soil. I pull it out, toss it into my weed bucket, and then begin again, unwinding the next vine from the next flower.

You might wonder why I don't pluck out the vines before they grow to the point of threatening to suffocate the entire garden. It's a valid question. But the truth is, I often don't recognize what's happening until it's almost too late. The vines are stealthy, creeping in and infiltrating my flower beds before I even notice they are there. They start out so innocuously, a slender thread draped here or there until, suddenly and seemingly all at once, their clutching tendrils have snaked every which way, trailing a carpet of green across the tops of the coneflower and the black-eyed Susans.

My metaphorical vine was like that too. I didn't recognize my work as a threat until it had permeated every aspect of my life and began to suffocate me. I didn't see I had a problem until I could no longer discern where my job as an author ended and where I began.

Sometimes it's impossible to disentangle the vine from the plant without killing them both. Like the thick vine stalks that had fused themselves to the trunk of my neighbor's pine tree, I wondered if my identity as an author had become so enmeshed with who I believed myself to be that I would be unable to separate the two. The pine tree had initially served as the scaffolding that allowed the vine to secure itself and grow, but now, observing how the two had become one, it seemed the roles had switched and the vine was supporting the tree. Was it in fact the vine that was holding *me* together too? Could I extract one from the other without destroying both? I didn't know.

I didn't know how to unwind the vine, and frankly, when I considered the possibility of doing that, it felt like a lot of work—work I wasn't sure I had the fortitude and patience for. Living with a familiar and, dare I say, comfortable misery felt less frightening and intimidating than stripping off the camouflage and stepping naked and vulnerable into the unknown.

Like the Israelites who lamented losing the "security" of their captivity in Egypt (Exodus 16:1–3), I too feared the barren wilderness of the unfamiliar. I knew how to be an author. I knew what the rhythm of my days looked like and felt like. I knew how to hustle and push. I didn't want to begin again. I certainly didn't relish the idea of standing naked, brittle, and vulnerable without the protection and security of the vine. And I couldn't help but wonder, *What if, under all that vine, there is nothing but a plain old boring pine tree?*

In the deepest part of me, I feared being ordinary. I was afraid of becoming invisible: a nobody. Being an author made me feel special and relevant, and my ego pushed hard against relinquishing that status. Writing had been my livelihood and passion for ten years; it was deeply fused into the heart of my identity. I wanted so badly to find a way to be my whole, true self *and* still work as an author, and I tried my damnedest to make it work—to find a way for the vine and the tree to coexist in harmony, without one killing the other.

Of course, you need only look at the pine tree in my neighbor's yard to know how this story will end every single time. No matter the extent of the pine tree's efforts, the obvious truth is that nothing short of cutting off the vine entirely will save it. The tree and the life-leaching vine cannot peacefully coexist. There is no possibility of a symbiotic relationship there. It was one or the other, and the choice was all mine.

As Benner writes, "Paradoxically, our fulfillment lies in the death of our own agendas of fulfillment. It also lies in the crucifixion of all our ego-centered ways of living apart from complete surrender to God. It does not lie, then, in any of the places we would expect to find it."[3] I learned, after much failure, that staying whole and healthy in my chosen vocation was not simply a matter of willpower. It wasn't about trying harder or trying something different. It also wasn't about surrender—or I should say, about the kind of surrender I wanted. I wanted "surrender" to be something I could do without making a sacrifice. True surrender, I ultimately came to understand, always entails a sacrifice because it entails death.

"We stick to the wrong thing quite often, not because it will come to fruition by further effort, but because we cannot let go of the way we have decided to tell the story," acknowledges David Whyte. "We become further enmeshed even by trying to make sense of what entraps us, when what is needed is a simple, clean breaking away."[4] Sometimes that which holds us captive has a stronger hold on us than anything else. For a long time, my desire to be known and valued by the world supplanted my desire to be known by God. I was in love with that which enslaved me. I loved the very vine that was leeching me of abundant life, and the story I'd decided to tell myself was that I needed this vine to find fulfillment.

But, as Thomas Merton asked, "How can I receive the seeds of freedom if I am in love with slavery? How can I cherish the desire of God if I am filled with another and opposite desire?"[5] I was in love with affirmation and success, and I turned toward it like a bewitched lover again and again, even when I knew my attachment was unhealthy—even when I knew my attachment had become idolatry. My need for love and belonging and my desire for affirmation and success consumed me, just like the vine consumed my neighbor's pine tree.

Maybe, for you, it's something—or someone—else you have wound around yourself. Maybe it's not your job or your calling or a need for affirmation and success that is consuming you, like it was for me, but a relationship, a status, an addiction, a belief, or even a bad habit. Whatever your "vine" is, you will eventually come to understand that nothing short of the death of that vine will save you. The question is, are you willing to give it up? Are you willing to give up the relationship, the status, the addiction, the belief, the bad habit? Are you willing to give up, as Whyte says, the way you've decided to tell your story? In other words, do you trust God enough to let go of that which you've looked to as the source of your identity?

The hard truth is, it's not easy to let go of the way we've decided to tell our story—particularly if we've been telling ourselves the same story for a long time. I knew in the deepest part of myself that Brad had declared the truth to me on that snowy February afternoon. And yet, I still didn't know if I could let go of the very thing that was causing me more sorrow than joy.

# CHAPTER TWO

# Gingko and Pin Oak

*When we know deep-down that something isn't
working, there's also a part of us that knows
what it's going to take to make the thing work
again. Likely it's going to take a death.*

LEEANA TANKERSLEY

One fall morning I noticed a spectacular gingko tree as I was walking to my office building. Even as I slid my key card into the door, I continued to stare over my shoulder at the captivating tree. Every one of the gingko's fan-shaped leaves shimmered a deep, rich shade of gold. Bright and vibrant in the warm autumn sun, the tree glowed as if it were lit from within.

Three hours later I slipped out the same door to run an errand during lunch and stopped dead in my tracks, aghast. The gingko tree was completely bare. Beneath its naked branches, a carpet of golden leaves fanned out like a Christmas tree skirt in a perfect circle at the base of its trunk. In a mere three hours, every leaf had dropped from the tree onto the grass below it.

During autumn, in preparation for their winter hibernation, most deciduous trees begin to close the veins that carry sap to their leaves. Over a period of weeks, as daylight slowly decreases and the temperature slowly cools, the tree produces a protective layer of cells that forms a barrier at the spot where each leaf stem connects to the branch. It's this barrier that eventually prompts the tree to drop the leaf, usually with the help of a breeze.[1] The first leaves to fall are those most exposed to the cold air at the top of the tree. Once the upper branches are bare, the leaves on the lower branches become exposed, prompting them to make their cell barriers and eventually fall too. Ultimately a hard frost often finishes the job, causing the last of the leaves to be released from the tree.

Gingko trees are deciduous in that they, too, drop their leaves in the fall. But rather than forming the cell barriers a few a time, the leaf stems on gingko trees all form their barriers at the same time and then patiently wait for the first cold snap, which signals the tree to drop its leaves all at once—usually over a period of a few hours, rather than days or weeks. On the day I discovered the denuded ginkgo tree, the morning weather had been warm. By the time I left at lunch, however, a sudden cold front had blown in, and the plummeting temperature alerted the gingko that it was time to let go of its leaves.

On the other end of the deciduous spectrum are species like the pin oaks and the beeches, which engage in what's called *marcescence*: a process that delays the formation of the barrier cells until much later in the season. Marcescence enables these trees to hold onto their leaves much longer than other trees, sometimes even through the entire winter and into early spring.

The pin oak in my backyard is the bane of my existence for this very reason. Long after the leaves of the river birch, crab apple, and honey locust trees have fallen, been raked up, and bagged, the oak tree remains fully clothed. Most years this particular tree doesn't let go of its leaves until December or January, which means you'll often find me bundled in my warmest clothes on a frigid winter day, grumbling as I rake, my fingers numb, my nose red and running. I love our regal pin oak tree, but I do not love raking its thousands of finally-fallen leaves in the middle of a Nebraska winter, when I'd rather be tucked into my couch, sipping hot, sugary tea and turning the pages of a good novel.

Scientists don't know for sure why some trees let go of their leaves in the fall while others engage in marcescence and hang onto their leaves for longer. Some botanists hypothesize that the dead, dry leaves help to camouflage tender twigs and buds, protecting them from hungry deer. Others suggest that dropping the dead leaves later creates a layer of compost on the ground at the base of the tree, which might provide nutrients helpful to spring growth.

One fact that scientists do agree on, however, is that by the time early spring arrives, the swelling buds and tiny leaves that form on the twigs and branches eventually force the few remaining dead leaves to the ground. Whatever is no longer useful to the tree ultimately falls away so that new life can emerge in its place. This, it turns out, is a useful metaphor as we consider what we might need to release along the journey of becoming who we are.

### *Letting Go like a Gingko, Letting Go like an Oak*

Sometimes when it comes to deciding whether to let go of something in our lives—a job, a habit, a relationship, a belief, a failure, a disappointment, a grief, an anger—we are quickly able to identify and release what is no longer serving us. We weigh our options, get our affairs in order and then, like the gingko tree, we let go of what we no longer need quickly and all at once. During other seasons and in other circumstances, however, we can be more like the maple—letting go bit by bit, leaf by leaf. And sometimes we are the pin oak in my backyard. We clutch tight-fisted to our leaves, reluctant to release.

In her book *Maybe You Should Talk to Someone*, psychologist Lori Gottlieb outlines five stages of decision-making.[2] When I look back, I can clearly see how each of Gottlieb's stages played out in my own decision to quit book-writing. Turns out, I was much more like the pin oak than the gingko tree. I clutched my leaves, stagnating in Gottlieb's stage one—what she calls "pre-contemplation"—for years. I complained, lamented, wallowed, and generally felt miserable about my work without ever fully admitting to myself that I was miserable.

Brad's observation that book-writing had brought me far more sorrow than joy finally launched me into the second of Gottlieb's stages of decision-making: contemplation. And yet, though I knew Brad had spoken the truth that February afternoon, the fact that I was contracted to write another book was, understandably, a major impediment to my willingness to let my job go.

For starters, there was the obvious money problem. If I withdrew from the contract, I knew I would be obliged to pay back the advance I had received from the publisher to write the book. This was not something I was eager to do for several reasons, not least of which was the fact that the advance money had long been spent.

I fantasized about my agent calling to tell me that, due to weak sales of my most recent book, the publisher was sorry but, regrettably, they would be forced to release me from my contract to write another book. In short, I fantasized about being fired. This, to me, was the perfect solution. If I were fired, I'd get to keep the advance—I could tell myself it was a severance pay of sorts—I wouldn't have to write a book I didn't want to write, and I wouldn't have to deal with the shame of actually quitting. I'd be off the hook. In my mind, getting fired was, ironically, the best way for me to "save face."

And "saving face" was very important. I am the daughter of an Army drill sergeant. Growing up, the mantra repeated in my household most often was, "Make it happen." In other words, I was taught from a very young age that you don't quit, no matter what. You soldier on. You power through. You do what needs to be done, and you gut it out until the job is done right. To quit is to fail; to quit is to admit weakness. Quitting is not an option.

More than forty years later, quitting anything—particularly a job, even when that job is clearly making me miserable—is still anathema to me. I simply did not consider quitting—withdrawing from my book contract—to be an option. And yet, here's the thing: every time I attempted to settle down and get to work on writing the book I was contracted to write, I found myself engaging in all sorts of stall tactics. I scrubbed tile grout in the guest bathroom. I repotted eleven succulents into matching white ceramic pots. I organized the kitchen utensils in the drawer according to size, shape, and color. The books I'd ordered for research sat collecting dust in a stack on the floor next to my desk. The chapter outline I'd drafted languished in a rarely opened folder on my laptop.

On the few occasions I forced myself to sit at my desk, I found I couldn't bring myself to type a single word. My brain froze, refusing to conjure sentences. I awoke every morning with a pit in my stomach. My neck ached, my jaw was permanently clenched, and the muscles in my arms and legs twitched on and off all day. It was as if my body was refusing to comply with what my mind demanded.

Prickly questions pinged around the inside of my brain day and night. *Will my lackluster attitude impact my ability to write a compelling book,* I wondered? *Will readers be able*

*to tell somehow that my heart isn't in it? Is it even right—
ethical, moral, Christian, for heaven's sake—to force myself
through the motions of producing a book simply to fulfill my
obligation to the publisher?*

The answer was clear. My body was telling me what I
needed to do even before my brain was ready to accept the
truth. In the deepest part of myself, I knew that writing a
book I truly did not want to write would be disingenuous
both to readers and to myself, and yet, I could not bring
myself to listen to what I already knew, because I could not
bring myself to withdraw from the contact. I could not bring
myself to quit.

"They definitely want you to write the book," my agent
insisted. At my request, she'd initiated a delicate conversation
with my editor about the possibility of withdrawing from the
contract, and she had called me to report on the outcome of
the call. "In fact," she added, "they're really excited about it
and are looking forward to reading the manuscript."

"So there's no chance they'll fire me?" I asked her, hopefully.

"There's no chance they'll fire you," she confirmed.

It was clear: if I was going to extricate myself from this
contract, I was going to have to be the one who cut the cord.
I knew this was what I needed to do, and yet, I couldn't.
I wasn't "the kind of person who broke a contract." I was
responsible. I was a professional. I was reliable, trustworthy,
and committed. I was not a quitter. Therefore, I couldn't
possibly break my contract. The problem was, I also couldn't
possibly write this book.

### Your Work Is Not Your Identity

"So tell me, what are you risking if you break this book contract?" my friend Deidra asked me one day after I'd confided

my conundrum to her. "What values have you attached to it?" she probed. "What is it at the core of you that says you shouldn't or can't break this contract?"

Deidra's questions helped me recognize that I had attached the value of my own character and self-image to the book contract itself. A rule-follower to the core (remember: drill sergeant's daughter) as well as a type A, firstborn, Enneagram Three, I prided myself on my credibility, professionalism, reliability, and ability to get things done.

I had committed to write a book. I had signed my name on a line beneath my publisher's. I had a copy of the contract in the file cabinet next to my desk. Therefore it was my duty to see the project through. If I bailed, I'd be an irresponsible, unprofessional, unreliable, and untrustworthy person. Bailing on the contract would not only mean I was a failure and a quitter, it would also mean I was a bad person.

Psychologists use the term *enmeshment* to describe a situation in which the boundaries between two people become blurred, resulting in loss of identity for one or both of the people in the relationship.[3] A child who is deeply enmeshed with her mother, for example, might become unable to distinguish her own thoughts and feelings from what she believes her mother thinks and feels. In families, enmeshment can lead to a dysfunctional relationship between the parent and the child, with the child often experiencing a loss of control and feelings of inauthenticity, resentment, and shame.

Enmeshment, it turns out, can also happen when our sense of self (who we are) becomes entangled with our work (what we do). This might not be a terrible thing if our work is going well. But we'll likely face a painful identity crisis if we are fired or laid off, or if we just plain quit a job that has become enmeshed with our identity.

My self-identity was deeply enmeshed with my work as a writer. Thankfully, Deidra's insightful questions helped me separate my identity from the act of withdrawing from my book contract. Breaking my book contract—in essence, quitting my career—I finally came to understand, didn't define who I was as a person and a professional. The decision didn't make me a "good person" or a "bad person." Rather, the decision to break my book contract was simply indicative of the fact that my life had taken an unexpected turn to which I was responding in the best, most authentic way possible. In the end, I realized, quitting was actually the truest choice I could make.

After I had successfully navigated the pre-contemplation and contemplation stages of decision-making, I was able to walk through Gottlieb's stage three—preparation—and stage four—action—relatively quickly and easily. My husband and I were prepared together to take the step. I negotiated with my boss at my part-time job to increase my hours. My agent arranged the "Termination of Contract Agreement" with my publisher. I signed the paperwork and mailed it back with a check for the amount I'd been paid for the advance. I even posted an Instagram photo of me holding my signed termination contract.

It was official. I'd hacked off the vine. I fired myself from the job I knew was not good for me. I released what was suffocating me and inhibiting me so that I could begin, I hoped, to grow again.

It was finished…or so I thought. As I quickly learned, the fifth and last stage in Gottlieb's decision-making process—maintenance—is by far the most difficult. Turns out, after we finally gather the courage to sever the vine, letting go of whatever it is we've wound round and round ourselves, that thing that's been suffocating us and inhibiting our ability to live as our best selves, we are left to contend with what's underneath.

# CHAPTER THREE

# Weeping River Birch

*The stages of change are such that you don't drop
all of your defenses at the same time. Instead, you
release them in layers, moving closer and closer
to the tender core: your sadness, your shame.*

LORI GOTTLIEB

"I'm quitting. I'm breaking my book contract. I just told my agent a few days ago," I blurted to a group of writers gathered in Kentucky for a four-day retreat. Staring hard at the floor, unable to make eye contact as my declaration hung in the quiet air, I suddenly felt afraid. Afraid of being seen as weak. Afraid of being thought of as a quitter. Afraid of being judged. Part of me yearned for those in the circle around me to clamor in protest, to try to change my mind. "What? No! You can't quit!" I wanted them to shout in horror and dismay. I thirsted for their approval and affirmation. And yet, at the same time, in a deeper, quieter, more secret place in me, I simply yearned to be heard and understood. I needed their compassion. I needed to be consoled. I needed them to tell me everything was going to be okay.

Which is exactly what they did—sometimes with their words, but mostly simply with their quiet presence. These men and women whom I barely knew came alongside me and generously held space for me in one of my most tender, vulnerable moments. It was ironic, of course, that

I was attending this writer's retreat for the first time and announcing that I was quitting book-writing. But in the end, the retreat was the exact right place and time to name the secret I was carrying in my heart. At that retreat, in a small town deep in Kentucky horse country, I was met where I was with compassion. I was accepted in the midst of my bewilderment, disappointment, and sorrow. I was not deemed a quitter, a failure, or a fool. I was not judged. Instead, I was accepted with warmth and love exactly as I was in that moment—raw, exhausted, embarrassed, sad, and more than a little bit relieved.

Turns out, somewhere deep in myself I had known I needed to name my decision, to say it out loud and to hear what it would sound like and feel like in the presence of other people. Declaring my intention to others, particularly those who were not in my innermost circle, made it real. My decision to let go of my job and the identity I'd clutched so desperately for a decade needed to sit in the open, outside of myself, to be acknowledged by others.

Naming my desires and intentions alongside my fears in Kentucky gave me the courage and confidence to widen my circles of disclosure—first to close friends and confidants, then slowly, over time, to acquaintances and colleagues, and then finally to my readers. Inviting others into my decision helped to solidify it in a way that turning it round and round in my own mind couldn't. At the same time, naming my decision to quit book-writing also exposed me to the questions, curiosity, and disappointment of others.

### When Right Now Is What's Next

"So, what's next then?" my boss asked me the morning I told him about my decision to step away from book-writing. He stood at the threshold of my cubicle with his arms crossed, and though his question to me did not come as a surprise, my answer surprised him. "This," I said, gesturing vaguely to myself and my surroundings. "Right now is what's next."

I saw confusion and disappointment in his raised eyebrows and heard it in the pause that yawned open in the space between us. This, after all, was the same boss who always introduced me as a "published author with books on Amazon and in Barnes & Noble." When my boss laughed uncomfortably, perhaps unsure if I was joking and definitely not sure how to respond to my vague, unambitious answer, I felt a little like I was letting down my dad. I changed the subject so as not to prolong the awkwardness, but I knew my answer to his question was the truth—though I was as surprised as he was to hear myself say it. For the first time in as long as I could remember, I didn't have a "next." I had only right now.

Our culture demands that we always have our "what's next" all figured out. It's assumed the ladder goes in only one direction in our professional lives: up. We are expected to keep climbing. We are expected to have a one-year plan, a five-year plan, a ten-year plan. We are expected to have goals, a vision—to be ready with an acceptable answer when we're asked, "What's next?" It's the American way, right? We strive. We have ambition. We have our "what's next" lined up, and the path typically follows an upward trajectory.

For most of my life this is exactly how I've operated. I had the vision and the strategy. I plotted my professional path and methodically ticked through the necessary milestones to reach my goals. I've always lived with my heart, mind, and soul set on the future, with one foot in what's next and the other foot in what's next after that.

Admitting we don't have our "what's next" worked out is the antithesis of cultural expectations, especially when it comes to our professional lives. And yet, sometimes not having a "what's next" all figured out is the very best thing we can do, both for ourselves and our vocation. After I stepped out of the publishing arena, I was surprised to discover that what I most desired right then was to live with both feet firmly planted in the present. After spending most of my life chasing the next thing, I suddenly found myself craving the opposite. I yearned for anonymity and smallness. I desired gratifying but not necessarily publicly visible work. I wanted much less online communication and much more face-to-face connection, greater intimacy, and smaller circles. I felt incredible freedom and contentment in doing good but largely invisible work in my part-time job. It felt perfectly right to step back from the relentless push toward platform- and brand-building and try to live more intentionally in the seemingly mundane but surprisingly satisfying minutiae of my life.

From the outside, my life looked ordinary, boring even. I wrote fundraising copy for my part-time job. I refilled the bird feeders in my backyard and kept an eye out the sunroom windows for the Northern Flicker who tapped in rapid staccato at the suet. I shuttled teenagers to tennis lessons and study sessions. I walked the dog and emptied the dishwasher. And yet, I felt exhilarated and unexpectedly delighted by my contentment to "fill a small space," as Susanna Wesley once said. I didn't have a "what's next," and for the first time in my life, that felt exactly right.

### Sitting in Our Space

Part of the process of releasing what no longer serves us is learning to live in the space that opens in the aftermath. This isn't always easy or comfortable. Many of us have so thoroughly trained ourselves to produce and "do" and have so seamlessly enmeshed our self-image with what we achieve, we struggle hard to relinquish the striving, planning, and expecting in order to simply be present in the moment. I was no exception. Though I felt like a burden had been lifted, and I relished the freedom that came with having fewer goals and responsibilities after I stepped away from book-writing, at the same time, I pushed hard against the unfamiliar and often disorienting spaciousness in my life. The temptation was to fill that space with another project or goal, because that's what I had always done. It took effort and intention to sit in this new space—a space that would have once looked to me like failure, laziness, and uselessness—and not only be fully present in it but also to release my hopes and expectations for what this fallow period might produce.

Many of us let go of something only because we expect that we will gain something else as a result. We've heard the expression "Say no so you can say a better yes" and the adage "When God closes a door he opens a window." But the hard truth is, letting go of one thing doesn't necessarily create the opportunity for something better or even something else. Sometimes the dream, goal, job, or relationship needs to be released because it's no longer good for us, because it no longer aligns with who we are or even simply because, in spite of our best efforts to make it happen, it's not meant to be. Sometimes the whole point of letting go is not so we can fill the space that opens up in its wake with something else or something better, but so we can open *ourselves* more fully in that space.

As I write this, I'm sitting on my backyard patio in the shade of our seventy-five-foot pin oak tree. Unlike the white pine on the edge of my yard, whose branches climb like steps from the ground all the way up to the crown, this oak rises like an Ionic Greek column, unblemished and solid, with twenty-five feet or more of trunk between the ground and its lowest limb. The reason there are no limbs, branches, or leaves on the lower part of this pin oak is because at some point along the way, the tree has let them die.

As an oak tree grows, its limbs and branches continue to grow up and outward. As these new limbs and branches grow larger, they shade the branches below it, subsequently inhibiting the leaves on those lower branches from using photosynthesis to transform the light from the sun into nutrients. Over time, as their ability to photosynthesize diminishes, these lower leaves wither and die, and finally, the leafless branch itself breaks off from the trunk. Because it does not need them any longer and is better able to thrive without these weaker branches draining important nutrients and energy, the tree simply lets them go.

There is an important lesson for us here. Like the oak tree in my backyard, there are times in our lives when we realize that something we once desired or depended on is no longer useful or even healthy for our continued growth and development. It might even be getting in the way of our ability to grow further into who we are becoming. And so we allow this "branch" we no longer need to diminish on its own, or, when necessary, we prune it ourselves, lopping off that which is draining us of essential life and stunting our ability to grow and thrive.

Recently I discovered that the Greek word for "prune" is *kathairo*, which also means "to cleanse." We see the word *kathairo* in the Gospel of John: "He cuts off every branch of mine that doesn't bear fruit, and he *prunes* the branches that do bear fruit, so they will produce even more" (John 15:2 NLT, emphasis added). The word *catharsis*—which is defined as "the process of releasing, and thereby providing relief from, strong or repressed emotions"—comes from *kathairo*.

The Greek philosopher Aristotle famously wrote about the tragedy as a catharsis, a means to purge negative emotions, particularly sorrow and fear.

There is something refreshing and hopeful in this image of being cleansed of that which we no longer need or which does not belong. But don't let this definition of pruning fool you into thinking this process of letting go is easy. It's not. It's a kind of death. As Thomas Merton wrote, "In order to become myself I must cease to be what I always thought I wanted to be, and in order to find myself I must go out of myself, and in order to live I have to die."[1] If you're like me, you will endeavor to avoid this surrender—this death to self—through sheer willpower. And ultimately, only when you come to the very end of yourself will you truly surrender.

Recently I was having a conversation with a podcaster about my experience of quitting book-writing, and the person interviewing me said something I realized wasn't altogether true. "That was a really brave thing to do," she said. "Stepping away from your career as an author took a lot of courage." I hesitated for a couple of seconds, and then I responded with the truth. "It wasn't actually an act of courage," I said, "because it was a decision made from a place of absolute desperation."

The truth was, I had resisted what I knew I needed to do for a very long time. It wasn't until I had fallen into a complete state of disintegration and hit rock bottom mentally, spiritually, and physically that I finally decided to let go of that which was causing me such unhappiness and sowing so much discord in my life. It wasn't courage; it was basic self-preservation. My survival instinct took charge. I had come to the very end of myself, and in order to live, the part of myself I was most desperate to hold on to—my self-created identity as an author—had to die.

## A Tree Needs to Weep

Initially, the process of deciding whether or not to quit book-writing was much more difficult than actually living out the consequences of the decision. The very day I told my agent, once and for all, that I had decided to withdraw from my book contract, pay back the advance to the publisher, and step out of the publishing arena, I felt an immediate, instantaneous sense of peace and relief wash over me, and for weeks after, I felt nothing but wildly, exuberantly alive. No more social media! No more platform-building! No more obsessively checking Amazon ranks! No more branding! No more comparison and jealousy! I was free to live a good life as my very best self—relaxed, relieved, and happy. The sorrow and angst were finally behind me. Or so I thought.

A couple of months after terminating my book contract, I made an appointment with an orthopedist for a simple procedure on my elbow. I'd been dealing with minor tendonitis for several weeks, and when the MRI revealed a small tear (thank you, January resolution to start lifting weights), the specialist recommended I get an injection of platelet-rich plasma into the tendon to jump-start healing. He assured me the procedure would be simple and straightforward: he'd draw a couple vials of my blood, spin the vials in a centrifuge to separate out the platelets, and then reinject the extracted platelets back into the tendon at the source of the injury. The in-office procedure would take less than an hour. Having already had surgery a few years before for a torn tendon in my left elbow, and living through the multi-week recovery period with my arm in a cast from wrist to bicep, I was more than willing to give this less-invasive option a go.

I admit, I typically get a little anxious when it comes to medical procedures, but strangely, I wasn't nervous at all as I lay on the exam table in the small, dim room. The nurse hadn't even asked me to undress and put on a gown. I'd merely pulled my arm from the sleeve of my sweater and laid back with my head on a pillow. "You're going to feel some pressure," the doctor murmured, and then he inserted a needle full of my own platelets into my elbow. As it turned out, "some pressure" was the understatement of the millennium. What I actually felt during the five-minute injection was teeth-gritting, fist-clenching agony.

By the time the short procedure was over, hot tears were streaming out of my eyes and running along my hairline and down my neck, where they dripped one at a time, slowly and steadily like fluid in an IV bag, onto the white sheet beneath me. Much to my surprise, once the tears started, they wouldn't stop, even after the doctor had finished with the procedure. Clearly neither he nor the nurse knew quite what to make of my stoically silent but persistent weeping. The nurse thrust a fist full of tissues into my hand as I lay splayed on the exam table. The doctor advised an ice pack, two Extra Strength Tylenol, and limited elbow movement. And then they both fled, urging me to "take my time," before pulling the door closed with a quiet click.

I wept as I slipped my throbbing arm back into the sleeve of my sweater, retrieved my purse from the hook, and gingerly slipped it over the shoulder of my good arm.

I wept as I hurried through the waiting room, chin tucked to my chest, hair shielding my red-rimmed eyes so as not to startle the patients awaiting their own appointments.

I wept as I drove home, wrangling the steering wheel with one hand.

I was still weeping when, back in the privacy of my own living room, I tucked myself into the corner of the sofa, cradling my elbow with a cupped palm.

It was only then that I began to wonder if I might be crying over something other than my elbow, painful though it was.

Earlier that morning I had published a blog post about my decision to quit book-writing. This blog post had been a long time coming. I'd told my family and friends; I'd told my coworkers and a few writer friends; but I hadn't yet made "the big announcement" to my readers, many of whom had supported me through all four of my previous book releases and had been reading my blog since its inception ten years prior. As I sat in the orthopedist's waiting room before being called back for my appointment, I pulled the post up on my phone to read some of the comments that had begun to pour into my website.

I didn't expect any "big feelings." Though I published the post about my decision that morning, I'd made the actual decision many weeks before. I knew there was a little bit of sadness there—I even named it "grief" in the post—but mostly what I felt as I wrote the blog post was a continuation of the relief and unburdening I'd experienced since the day I signed and mailed the "Termination of Contract" agreement.

Until, that is, the orthopedist's needle pricked something far beneath flesh and tendon. What began as a tearful reaction to unexpected physical pain crossed an invisible threshold. My tears at the sudden, sharp stab of the needle deep in the soft tissue of my elbow opened a portal of sorts into which I tumbled headlong. The tears prompted by the unexpected jolt of searing pain opened a way for me to feel the sorrow and loss I had acknowledged in words but hadn't actually allowed myself to feel.

Enneagram experts say that we Type Threes—"The Achievers/Performers"—are the least aware of and in touch with our feelings. Until recently I would have told you that I am a person who is very in touch with my feelings, thank you very much. After all, I write personal essays on my blog, right? I've written two memoirs, right? Of course I'm in touch with my feelings! Turns out, this is not entirely true.

I first began to suspect I'd been fooling myself when a podcast host informed me that, in preparation for his upcoming interview with me, he had read my blog from start to finish, from the very first post I wrote in July 2008 to the post I had published that very week. Can I just say, there is no more horrifying realization than hearing someone say they have read every word of your blog? Suddenly I felt as if I was sitting at my desk stark naked. But what he said next was in some ways worse. "You're a very private person," he declared. "You don't reveal a whole lot." *Wait, what?* Truly, this was news to me. I thought of myself as very transparent in my online writing, very authentic and vulnerable. The podcaster saw what I was doing with my public writing before I saw it myself.

I have come to see that I used the process of writing publicly on my blog and on social media as a way to distance myself from my own feelings, to let myself off the emotional hook. I believed—or perhaps wanted to believe—that writing about my feelings in these public spaces was the same as feeling my feelings. I understand now, however, that writing about my experiences and even naming my feelings publicly does not necessarily mean I have truly taken the time and space to actually feel: to wade with my whole mind, body, and soul into difficult emotions like grief, anger, shame, and disappointment and allow myself to experience the confusing, uncomfortable, unkempt, uncertain mess of these difficult feelings. Writing about a painful experience—even writing about it with seeming transparency and emotional depth—is not the same as living through and feeling the many nuanced emotional facets of that experience over time.

*

Several years ago, we noticed the river birch tree in our backyard was dripping what looked like water down its trunk. A quick Google search informed us that the "water" was actually sap, which was being released from the spot on the trunk where Brad had pruned off a large branch the week before. Initially I was concerned. It didn't seem like a good sign that our tree was pouring sap from its wound, and I wondered if we should apply some sort of sealant over the spot where we had made the cut in order to staunch the flow and protect the tree from infection.

I've since learned that sealing a pruning wound is actually one of the worst things a gardener can do to a tree. In recent years, scientists have discovered that pruning sealants, once a popular remedy, actually do more harm than good because they obstruct a tree's natural healing power and can trap moisture in the tree, which can potentially lead to infection and decay.[2]

Some trees "weep" or "bleed" from their wounds more than others, and in fact, the river birch belongs to a group of trees often referred to as "bleeder trees" for their propensity to release prodigious quantities of sap from their pruning wounds.[3] A pruned tree literally needs to "weep" in order to heal when it is wounded. It's best to leave its raw wound open to the air and the elements. Covering the wound and blocking this release—sealing in the sap that needs to be bled out—is ultimately detrimental to the tree's ability to heal from this wound, as well as other aspects of its long-term health.

The same can be said of us. We often try to "seal in" our pain too. Our human inclination is to distract ourselves from, numb, or bury our pain—anything so we won't actually have to feel it. Though seemingly easier and less painful at the outset, in the long run, distracting ourselves from our pain with busyness; numbing it with alcohol, scrolling, Netflix binges, or shopping; displaying it for public consumption (like I did by publicly writing about my sorrow) before we have properly processed it ourselves, either alone or with a trusted confidante; or sealing it within ourselves by refusing to acknowledge it only thwarts our ability to heal and thrive in the long-term.

We need to feel the pain of our wounds and engage in the cathartic process of release in order to heal and, ultimately, thrive as our best selves. It's hard and deeply uncomfortable to feel emotional pain. And yet, the only path to true healing, growth, and transformation is to do exactly what we most want to avoid: to step into the pain and stay in it for as long as it takes the wound to heal. As so many wise people have said, the only way out of grief is through it.

After the unexpected ungluing in the orthopedist's office and the subsequent realization that I had some emotional work to do, I spent the rest of the week quietly and slowly reading through every beautiful, heartfelt, kind, loving, and encouraging email, blog post comment, Facebook message, and tweet I'd received in the wake of my announcement about quitting book-writing. My inclination was to rush through this process—to skim over these notes of kindness, empathy, and compassion. I wanted to read through them fast, to get it over with in order to keep myself at arm's length from whatever emotions might begin to bubble uncomfortably to the surface.

But I didn't do that this time. Instead, I read each message slowly and thoughtfully. As I read, I let myself receive and feel my sorrow and my grief. I let my wound stay uncovered and open. I stayed in the feelings and leaned more fully into them—into their messy unruliness and into their stubborn refusal to be managed and contained.

"Knowing what we feel is the first step to knowing why we feel that way," writes Bessel Vander Kolk in his best-selling book *The Body Keeps the Score*.[4] "Knowing what we feel," sounds obvious, doesn't it? And yet, the truth is, we *don't* always know what we are feeling because we don't allow ourselves to feel our feelings in the first place. Feelings can be scary. They can be uncomfortable. They can force us to face things we'd rather avoid—things like disappointment, shame, and failure. And so often, we do everything in our power to not feel. We distract ourselves with our to-do lists. We buy a new purse. We numb ourselves with Netflix. We scroll and scroll and scroll.

When my body forced me to feel my sorrow and grief, I was able to acknowledge that the story I had written for myself in my hopes and dreams all those years ago when I began to write my first book didn't ultimately write itself in real life the way I had imagined and hoped. I acknowledged that while there had been joyful chapters along the way, there were also many chapters full of sorrow, disappointment, bitterness, resentment, anger, and frustration. I let myself feel the heartbreak of a broken dream. I let myself feel the disappointment, the bitterness. I let myself feel the grief that came in letting go of the story and the happy ending I had hoped for.

The spaciousness that opens up when we let go of something can hold our emotional pain—if we let it. That's why it's so critical that we not rush to fill that empty space with something else. If we don't hold space for it, emotional pain will tuck itself deep inside us, either biding its time for an opportunity to present itself or festering into an even deeper wound.

Emotional pain is both patient and stubborn. Ultimately it will use any channel available—including the orthopedist's needle—to make itself known and felt. It cannot be dulled with distraction forever, nor will it simply disappear if we keep it tamped down long enough. Where there is a death, there is emotional pain, and that pain will make itself known and felt, in spite of our best efforts to thwart it, suppress it, or ignore it.

Grief and other uncomfortable emotions can convey important information to us about our own selves and about who we are becoming—if we listen to and heed what they are telling us, that is. We'll explore this idea more in Chapter 10, but for now, let me simply say that naming difficult emotions—sorrow, disappointment, grief, anger, shame—both to others and to ourselves is a critical part of the journey toward growth and transformation. I wish it had not taken the sharp pierce of a needle for me to access and process my deep sorrow, but I am grateful for the healing I ultimately experienced as a result.

# CHAPTER FOUR

# Compost and Soil

*The soul must be continuously nourished or, like
the body, it becomes weak and malnourished.*

SUE MONK KIDD

We are lucky here in Nebraska. Winter arrives late, which means we often enjoy warm days into November. By the tail end of autumn, however, the days are noticeably shorter and cooler; most of the vibrant leaves have browned and fallen from the trees; and our vegetable garden is an unkempt mess of withered plants, desiccated vines, and shriveled herbs. Armed with shears, shovels, hoes, and rakes, Brad and I wrangle our two complaining teenagers into the backyard garden to clean up the beds and prepare the space for winter.

The four of us work furiously all day, yanking up the dead plants by the roots and tossing them one by one onto the compost pile—tomato vines still heavy with hardened, green fruit; wizened bell peppers that never quite ripened; towering sunflower stalks, their giant, drooping heads picked clean of seeds by the neighborhood finches and chickadees. We thrust our pitchforks deep into the hard-packed dirt, working methodically up and down the length of the raised beds, turning over the soil and adding shovelfuls of nutrient-rich compost as we go. Finally, the beds weeded and raked clean, the soil turned and "fed," our muscles aching and our palms blistered, we head indoors to wait out winter while the garden sleeps.

Anyone who has a backyard garden knows that preparing it for winter is some of the least fun, least rewarding work of the year. This late-fall labor involves none of the hopeful expectancy of spring planting. It produces none of the abundance of harvest—colanders full of fresh greens wet with the morning dew; fistfuls of fuchsia radishes, dirt still clinging to their roots; an apron-bowl of sun-warmed cherry tomatoes plucked fresh from the vine. Cleaning up the garden at the season's end is a chore. Turning over the soil by hand is dirty, back-aching work. Compost is messy. And at the end of the day, not only do we not have anything beautiful or tasty to show for our labor, we have to wait for months to reap the benefits of our efforts.

In the parable of the sower, Jesus told the crowd about a farmer who went out to sow his seeds. Some of the seeds the farmer sowed fell on the path, where they were eaten by the birds, Jesus explained. Some were scattered onto rocky places, but because there was little soil there, the plants that grew did not root deeply enough and were scorched by the sun. Other seeds fell among the thorns, which choked the tender plants when they sprouted. Finally, Jesus told his listeners, some of the farmer's seeds landed on good soil, "where it produced a crop—a hundred, sixty or thirty times what was sown" (Matthew 13:8 NIV).

Poet and author Luci Shaw notes that in this parable, it's not the seeds that change as the story unfolds, but the soil.[1] The farmer scatters the same seeds, but the seeds land on four different terrains. Those that fall on the hard-packed path, the ones that tumble into crevices between the rocks, and the ones that become entangled with the crowded, thorny plants do not have the proper sustenance to survive. On the other hand, Jesus tells us, the seeds that germinate in the good soil produce an abundant crop. In other words, the key to healthy growth and an abundant harvest begins with good soil. And the makings of good soil begin not in the spring, when tender sprouts are already pushing toward the warmth of the sun, but in the late fall and winter, when it seems like nothing is happening in the garden at all.

As I struggled with the decision to step out of publishing and break free from the suffocating grip of the vine, I could feel that I was unbalanced and out of sorts, though at the time, I couldn't put my finger on exactly why. Preparing my garden for winter reminded me of where I'd gone wrong. I'd neglected my soil. In putting nearly all my attention, energy, and resources toward maintaining the voracious vine for so long, I had leached myself of the nutrients needed to sustain the tree.

This neglect manifested itself in my body, mind, and spirit as physical, emotional, spiritual, and creative exhaustion. This is why, when I put my fingers to the keyboard to try to begin to write the book I was under contract to write, there was nothing there. Not a word. This is also why I felt so fragmented inside myself and so disconnected from everything and everyone. I had not tended to my soul. I had ignored it, starved it and abused it. And by the time I realized what I had been doing to myself, I was already critically depleted.

What I've learned the hard way from my experience is that we ignore our soul at our own peril. When we leach our soul dry—when we don't listen to and observe what it needs; when we don't tend to it, care for it, nourish it, and sustain it—our mind, body, and spirit suffer as a result. When we ignore our soul, we disintegrate physically, emotionally, spiritually, and creatively. The good news is that a depleted soul, like depleted soil, can be amended. Like compost feeds the garden soil at the end of the growing season, our souls can be fed. Over time, they can be brought back to life.

As Shaw points out, "This is no quick and easy fix. The best fertilizers are not the chemical additives alone but the organic manure or compost that works slowly and deeply into the soil of our lives as they are watered by the Spirit."[2] At the end of a productive gardening season, we mix rich compost into the soil, and then we let it rest, waiting through the long winter months for the nutrients to do their nurturing work. We can do the same with the soil of our own soul.

### Learning How to Feed Our Soul

One afternoon, a book on a display table caught my eye as I was roaming Barnes & Noble's aisles. Many years earlier I'd borrowed a copy of Julia Cameron's *The Artist's Way* from the public library and had read it cover to cover, but at the time, I'd mostly rolled my eyes as I read, dismissing the book as too "woo-woo" for me. I'd returned it to the library and didn't think about the book again until the afternoon, years later, when I spotted it displayed in the bookstore.

Against my better judgment and despite the fact that I'd already read the book and deemed it unhelpful, I bought *The Artist's Way* that day in Barnes & Noble. Over the course of twelve weeks, I not only re-read every word, I also did the exercises Cameron suggested. I've heard people say that sometimes a book is or is not right for us depending on the season of life we are in; *The Artist's Way* was such a book for me. What didn't work the first time I read it hit all the right notes the second time around.

*The Artist's Way* is a hands-on workbook intended to help writers, artists, musicians, and other creatives reactivate their creative energy and flow. Cameron swears by what she calls Morning Pages—a daily stream-of-consciousness journaling exercise (specifically, three notebook pages written long-hand)—and Artist Dates, in which once a week, you take yourself on a creative outing, like a visit to an art gallery or a museum or a walk in a nature sanctuary. In addition to these foundational exercises, Cameron also tackles a particular creative challenge or "block" in each chapter, addressing topics like "Recovering a Sense of Safety," "Recovering a Sense of Identity" and "Recovering a Sense of Possibility."

Each morning for twelve weeks I diligently wrote three longhand Morning Pages in my journal, and each weekend I dedicated an hour to journaling through Cameron's probing questions and prompts. After a few weeks of immersing myself in these practices, I began to awaken to a surprising, even shocking fact: I realized I didn't really know what enlivened or nourished me. I didn't know what brought me joy or delight. I didn't know what my dreams and desires were. I didn't know what I liked to do for fun (except read). I couldn't recall what I'd loved to do as a kid (besides read). In other words, I did not know how to feed my soul.

I was newly pruned, finally free of the vine and the relentless drumbeat of production, and I did not recognize myself. After letting go of most of what had consumed me and defined me, I didn't recognize what—or rather, who—was revealed, the real person who had been hidden for so long beneath the tangle of the vine. I was stunned to realize I had no idea who I was or what I liked to do when I wasn't working. *What do I like to do for fun?* I wondered. *What do I enjoy? If I had a whole free day to myself, how would I spend it?* I didn't have a clue.

Peering under the surface of myself was like opening my eyes underwater. The landscape of my inner self was blurry. Cameron assured me in her book that this fuzziness, these questions and vagueness, were a normal part of self-discovery. "Remember that the more you feel yourself to be *terra incognita,* the more certain you can be that the recovery process is working," she writes. "You are your own promised land, your own new frontier."[3] I Googled *terra incognita* to be sure I understood its meaning. It's Latin for "land unknown," and at one time was a term used by cartographers for regions that had not been mapped or documented. This felt right to me. I was uncharted territory.

*The Artist's Way* helped me reignite my creativity, but, even more importantly, it helped me begin to uncover who I am and how I can best nourish my soul. For example, one of Cameron's suggested journaling exercises entailed making a list of twenty favorite activities, along with the date of the last time you engaged in that particular activity. Armed with a brand-new journal and my favorite pen, I took myself on an Artist's Date to my favorite local coffee shop, opened to the first blank page, and jotted down this list:

1. Reading
2. Walking/hiking in nature
3. Photography
4. Gardening
5. Having dinner with Brad and/or friends
6. Swimming in a warm, outdoor pool
7. Sitting outdoors and observing nature
8. Browsing in a used bookstore
9. Shopping at consignment, thrift, and antique stores
10. Napping
11. Exploring a new place
12. Refurbishing and painting old furniture

You'll notice my list contains twelve, not twenty, activities. I sat at the corner table in the coffee shop for a full thirty minutes with my new journal splayed open on the table, but even with ample time, I simply couldn't come up with more than twelve activities I enjoyed doing. *That's okay,* I reassured myself. *Twenty is a lot. Twelve is good. Twelve is fine.* The clincher, though, was when I realized that aside from reading, gardening, and walking the dog (Does walking the dog even count as "walking/hiking in nature"? I'm not sure. Most days it felt more like a chore.), I couldn't remember the last time I'd actually done any of the things I claimed I enjoyed.

*Why don't I do the things I love?* I wrote under my list, underlining the question.

There are a lot of possible answers to that question: busyness, work, parenting, and household responsibilities among them, to be sure. But the real answer is simply that I'd forgotten. I'd forgotten what I enjoyed and what I liked to do for fun. I'd forgotten what energized me. I'd forgotten about the activities that enlivened me and fed me, the things that helped make me a whole, healthy, vibrant person. Seeing that list of twelve activities that brought me joy, I began to envision a fuller life for myself—a life that contained more than work, busyness, goals, deadlines, and responsibilities.

### Choose Life

For as long as I can remember, I've always been three steps ahead of myself. Striving to accomplish the next goal or meet the next milestone, I've tumbled from one project to the next, never pausing to consider whether I was enlivened by or and even enjoyed any of the activities that required such a tremendous expenditure of energy. When I finally did stop to reflect, I realized most of my previous ways of being and doing—producing books, articles, and blog posts; platform-building; speaking; social media; saying yes to things I didn't really want to do; striving; comparing—had been draining the life from me and driving me farther and farther away from my true self.

I had been so focused on striving to accomplish and achieve, pursuing recognition and success and pushing to gain approval and acceptance from those I admired, I'd neglected my own self. I'd sacrificed enjoyment, fun, and the activities that bring me life and make me feel like a whole, real person. My single-minded pursuit of what I'd hoped would bring me satisfaction had blinded me to that which truly makes me come alive. I'd thought, or maybe hoped, I could substitute one for the other. I'd thought, or maybe hoped, I could swap out what I actually loved with what I *wanted* to love. But it didn't work. My deepest, truest self couldn't thrive—or even survive—on the nutritionally vapid sustenance I was force-feeding it.

What I've learned through all of this is that I actually have a choice in how I want to live my life. I get to decide. I can choose life: I can choose to pursue the experiences that energize and enliven me. Or I can choose death: I can choose to pursue the experiences that drain and diminish me.

The writer of the book of Deuteronomy puts it this way: "I call heaven and earth to witness against you today that I have set before you life and death, blessings and curses. Choose life so that you and your descendants may live" (Deuteronomy 30:19 NRSV). As Christine Valters Paintner says, "Each choice allows us to move toward the things which bring us life. If we don't choose the path of growth, we can move toward that which drains us of life. The call of the pilgrim is to stay awake to our own patterns of life and death."[4]

Staying awake to our patterns of life and death sounds like a valuable and fruitful practice, but I know from experience that it's easier said than done. It takes deep intentionality not only to stay awake, but also to awaken initially to these life and death patterns—many of which are deeply ingrained in us—in the first place. So much can get in the way of both our awakening and our staying awake: busyness, distraction, expectations (our own and others'), depletion (physical, mental, or spiritual), fear, self-protection, our insecurities, and the formational experiences of our childhood.

Ironically, I think one of the reasons I stayed caught in the "death pattern" for so long was simply because I was too depleted to begin to make the hard choices and changes I knew I needed to make. I was too tired to care and in too deep to know where or how to begin to change my life.

It stands to reason that the more depleted we are, the less we are able to make the very choices that will begin to replenish and sustain us. I had poured a tremendous amount of energy into maintaining and trying to grow my career as an author—and, along with it, my false self. It took a lot of time, work, and energy to feed the vine, and when all was said and done, I had no resources left for the tree.

*The Artist's Way* not only helped me see how I was starving my true self, it also allowed me to recognize and remember what my soul needed to grow and thrive. I wrote the list of twelve life-giving activities, most of which I had neglected for years; it was right there in blue ink on the first page of my brand-new notebook. I saw that my soul was in desperate need of rich, loamy compost and a long, replenishing rest.

When we know ourselves, we are able to recognize and move toward the environments in which we thrive. Likewise, when we know ourselves, we are able to recognize and move away from the environments in which we fail to thrive. Some of us—maybe most of us—will become better at knowing ourselves through trial and error. Some of us will learn more quickly than others where and how we thrive and where and how we fail to thrive. Some of us will be stubborn. We will try to force ourselves to fit into a space or a place that is not right. We will try to change ourselves to fit our circumstances. Ultimately we will fail at this. And ultimately, in failing, we will come closer to knowing our true selves.

Turns out, the publishing industry was too big of an arena for me. The public nature of a career in publishing fed my voracious false self like gasoline feeds a fire. The more I looked to influencers in Christian publishing for approval and recognition and the more I pushed myself to be successful, admired, and known, the more my ego demanded and the more estranged I became from my true self, from the person God created me to be.

My false self did not miraculously vanish when I stepped out of the publishing arena. My desire for validation, affirmation, recognition, and success are still there. The difference is, this desire is not being fueled in the same way and to the same degree. I'm still a type A overachiever. I'm still a Three on the Enneagram. And these parts of myself, I understand now, are not inherently flaws. I still strive to be successful in my work as a writer at a nonprofit organization, and I still enjoy the validation I receive from my boss or my colleagues for work well-done. But because my work is not public in the same way, and the arena in which I am working is much, much smaller, my ego more easily stays in check. To be in a smaller and less visible space, I know now, is a healthier place for me.

In the aftermath of quitting my job, I have come to understand that there's nothing I could have done that would have better equipped me to succeed as a published author while at the same time keeping my self whole. I didn't "do it wrong." I didn't fail. Nor, as I said earlier, is the publishing industry "bad." Like a couple with irreconcilable differences, we—the publishing world and I—were simply not good together.

Still, I have no regrets. I haven't for a moment regretted my decision to leave publishing, nor do I regret the fact that

I entered into it. The fact is, as Parker Palmer so astutely says, "There are no shortcuts to wholeness."[5] I learned a lot about myself through the ups and downs of working in publishing for ten years, and I am still learning to recognize and embrace the whole of me—shadows and light, flaws and gifts. I am learning where I fit best—where I thrive and where I don't. I am learning to recognize my patterns of life and death. I am learning who I am, how to live as my best self and what a right-size life looks like for me.

### *Learning to Recognize Our "Right-Size" Life*

Our culture insists that more and bigger are always better—a bigger house, a bigger salary, a better job title, more stuff, more space, more money, more power. But the truth is, sometimes we thrive best in a smaller space with a lot less. Sometimes what's right for our heart, mind, and soul is a lot smaller—a lot less—than we what we've been taught by our culture to want or to expect.

If you've ever owned a houseplant, you probably know that as the plant grows, it needs to be transplanted into a larger pot from time to time to prevent its roots from becoming constricted in a too-small space. Given this, you might assume the bigger the pot, the better, right? After all, why waste time repotting a plant multiple times over the years as it grows when you can simply plant it once and for all in a large pot, where it will have plenty of space to grow over time.

Turns out, though, this isn't how it works—and not just because a tiny plant swallowed up by a huge pot would look ridiculous. The fact is, it's not healthy for a growing plant to have too much space. If a pot is too large, the ratio of roots to soil is too great for the roots to absorb all the moisture after watering. The extra moisture sits in the soil, eventually lead-ing to root rot which, if not caught in time, can kill the plant.

In other words, a plant needs the right-sized pot. A con-tainer that's too small will constrict the roots and inhibit growth, but a pot that's too large provides too much space, which can also ultimately be just as damaging to the plant's ability to grow and thrive. Despite what our culture insists, bigger and more isn't always better—neither better for our plants, nor better for our own selves. We are more like our houseplants than we might think: we need the right-sized pot to thrive.

Just like our plants tell us exactly what kind of container and soil they need to flourish, our souls will tell us too . . . if we listen. Mine did. Recently, as I was skimming through an old journal, I spotted a phrase that caught my eye at the top of the page. On January 15, 2019, I'd written a single sentence—"Live your right-size life"—directly under the date. It was the only thing I had written in my journal that day. I don't recall the context, or if it's a quote from some-one, or what may have prompted me to pen that directive to myself, fifteen days after my fourth book released and long before I began to recognize and acknowledge the vine. But my soul knew.

My soul knew even before I did that the life I'd made for myself—the life I was grasping at with all my strength, the life I was trying to fill with all my efforts and pushing and striving—was too big, too much, for me. "Live your right-size life," my soul whispered to me through the pages of my journal.

As we listen to what our soul already knows and begin to heed its desire for us, we will start to uncover the life that is the right size for us. When we nurture our right-size life and nourish our soil, we will begin to grow.

# PART 2

# Winter

## *Rest*

*Help us to always be hopeful*
*Gardeners of the spirit*
*Who know that without darkness*
*Nothing comes to birth*
*As without light*
*Nothing flowers.*

MAY SARTON

# CHAPTER FIVE

# Rose Bushes Wrapped in Burlap

*My plan is to live like the bears: to turn the compost a*
*few more times, prowl around a little longer and then*
*go to sleep until the white-throated sparrow, with its*
*coarse and cheerful song, calls me out of the dark.*

JANE KENYON

My neighbors two houses down when I was growing up
were avid gardeners. Every autumn, in addition to raking
their yard, pruning trees, and cleaning up flower beds and
their huge vegetable garden, they would wrap a swath of
burlap around each of the rose bushes that lined the front
walkway. Once each shrub was enveloped in its tent, they
filled the inside cavity with dead leaves and mulch, burying
the entire bush in a natural insulation of sorts. I was always
strangely comforted every November when I saw my neighbors' wrapped rose bushes, knowing the delicate twigs and
branches would be snug in their cozy burrows as the Massachusetts winter raged around us.

I know now that my neighbors wrapped their rose bushes
in burlap and buried them in leaves not only to protect the
delicate canes from snow and ice, but more importantly, to
keep the rose bushes at a consistent temperature throughout the winter, ensuring that they remained in a dormant
state for the entire season. A midwinter warm spell can be
dangerous to some types of roses and other plants because

it prompts them to bud too early and consequently suffer damage —called winterkill—when the temperature inevitably plunges to freezing again. Seasoned gardeners like my neighbors know that winter dormancy is just as critical to a plant's ability to thrive as the more fruitful spring and summer seasons.

Many early spring bulb flowers like tulips and daffodils also need this period of dormancy. If you've ever tried to "force" spring flowers into blooming early in a pot inside your house, you know that in order to bloom properly, the bulbs of these particular plants need a prolonged period of pre-chilling, usually in the back of your refrigerator, for several weeks. Exposing bulbs to the cold stimulates a biochemical response that initiates root growth and triggers flower formation. Without this forced period of dormancy, the bulbs will still try to bloom, but the flowers often end up stunted and malformed.

"Waning in particular is an essential energy in our lives," writes Christine Valters Paintner. "We live in a culture of perpetual waxing, of striving to do as much as possible and squeeze as much as we can into a day. Yet nature offers us a very different way of being."[1] I appreciate how Painter refers to waning as an "essential energy." Waning—resting—seems like the exact opposite of energy, doesn't it? But Paintner has helped me see that while it might not look or feel like the kind of energy or activity we are accustomed to in our 24/7, go-go-go lives, actively resting is indeed a kind of essential energy.

There is more—much more—going on under the surface of ourselves than meets the eye when we retreat into the winter of our souls. Like the rose bush wrapped in burlap and the tulip bulb chilling underground (or in the back of the fridge), we too need proper periods of dormancy in order to bloom to our fullest potential. As Paintner advises, we would be wise to "embrace the wisdom of both fruitfulness and fallowness."[2] It's in our best interest to surrender to, rather than resist, these dormant seasons, allowing adequate time to rest, restore, and refuel. The winter of our soul is a necessary waning—a period of physical and mental rest, a retreat from many of the demands of our noisy, bossy world.

## *Retreat*

Last night when I went to lower the blinds in our bedroom, I was surprised that I could see clear into our neighbor's yard. Obscured behind a wall of dense foliage seven months of the year, their house, tucked into the bare woods at the end of a long, curving driveway, was now plainly visible. As I stood at my second-floor bedroom window, I could see the bright light from their television spilling from their living room window, illuminating the snow outside. A Christmas tree in the corner twinkled a rainbow of colored lights.

"Why?" I asked my son Noah recently when he acknowledged that winter is his favorite season. Frankly, I am incredulous that anyone would choose what I consider the most barren, dark, and depressing time of the year as their favorite. Turns out, Noah loves winter for all the reasons I find this season unappealing: the starkness of the landscape, the monochromatic palette, its slowness and quiet and cold.

I will probably never come to love winter or elevate it to the status of my favorite season, but as I get older, I am better able appreciate a little of what Noah values about it. There is something about winter's sparseness that invites a sharper clarity. In the absence of the clutter and noise of fuller seasons, deeper questions and insights have more space to come into focus. There is a starkness to winter, both in the actual landscape and in the landscape of our souls, that enables us to see straight into the heart of things. Here, in winter, the essence of nature—and of ourselves—is revealed.

It just so happened that the winter of my soul coincided with actual winter in Nebraska. It doesn't always work this way. As Katherine May so astutely notes in her book *Wintering*, "Some winters happen in the sun."[3] And I would add that the opposite is true, too: some summers happen in the snow. Sometimes we enjoy our most fruitful periods during the coldest, darkest months and then find ourselves needing rest and replenishment come summer when the sun blazes and the world around us explodes with new life. The winter of my soul, however, happened as the days shortened and grew cold and the trees relinquished the last of their leaves. As the world outside my windows quieted, I quieted the noise of my own life. Like a fragile rose cane, I wrapped myself in metaphorical burlap and retreated into a long winter's rest.

One of the first things I did to quiet myself and my environment during this period of self-hibernation was to shut down my professional Facebook page and take a hiatus from my other social media accounts. I deleted the Instagram, Twitter, and Facebook apps from my phone so I wouldn't be tempted to take one quick peek, knowing I would spiral quickly back into mindless scrolling if given the opportunity. I didn't put any parameters around when, or if, I would return to social media. I simply shut it all down and gave myself permission to step away indefinitely.

This respite from social media was transformative, not only because it helped me kick my addiction to mindless scrolling, but also because the time and space that opened in its absence revealed the deeper reason I gravitate toward social media in the first place. The truth is, while my intentions to use social media to share beauty and encouragement are genuine, underneath those good intentions also lurks a more insidious motive: a quiet but persistent vying to be visible, heard, and relevant—an appeal for approval and affirmation. As psychologist Scott Barry Kaufman explains, stepping away from social media is a way to "quiet the ego"[4]—and truth be told, my ego is in constant need of quieting. As I hushed the external noise and the internal prodding of my own ego, I felt relief in embracing what Akiko Busch calls "the merits of the inconspicuous life"—the "value of going unseen, undetected [and] overlooked." Busch asks, "Might invisibility be regarded not simply as refuge, but as a condition with its own meaning and power?"[5]

Being inconspicuous or even invisible, Busch points out, "is not the equivalent of being nonexistent. It is not about denying creative individualism nor about relinquishing any of the qualities that make us unique, original, singular."[6] She looks to the natural world for evidence, where insects and animals use camouflage to protect themselves, hunt for prey, and attract a mate.

The Merveille du Jour moth, for instance, displays an intricate mosaic of grays and browns across its wings and body, so that one must look very closely to spot it on a bed of lichen. Geometrid caterpillars will freeze in place on a branch, extending their bodies outward to replicate the exact shape of a twig. The arctic hare, which lives in the harsh environment of the North American tundra, has a thick coat of brilliant-white fur during the winter that blends well with the snow and ice, but in the spring, the hare's fur turns blue-gray to reflect the shades of the surrounding rocks and vegetation. The bodies of leafy sea dragons off the coast of Australia are covered in yellow-brown leaf-like appendages that provide near-perfect camouflage amid the undulating seaweed and kelp. Invisibility in the natural world is "nuanced, creative, sensitive, discerning. Above all, it is powerful," says Busch.[7]

As I retreated from the public sphere of social media and into invisibility, I wrestled with the fear of being forgotten. My ego pushed hard against being "quieted." I didn't like this part of myself—it felt weak and needy and frankly kind of pathetic, and it was hard to acknowledge it. But it was important to accept not only that this insecurity existed in me but also that it was not the truest part of me. My fear of being overlooked and forgotten was not God-created, and as I began to understand that in the deepest part of myself, I began to be able to let it go.

In releasing my long-held fear of being unnoticed and forgotten, I began to experience an unexpected feeling not only of liberation but also of the power Busch writes about. Embracing invisibility allowed me to begin to find myself. Not the false self I tried so hard to be—ambitious, successful, and valuable for what I produced—but the self I really was underneath the shiny veneer of achievement. I was surprised to discover new facets of myself, like the fact that I am easily satisfied and that I actually thrive in simplicity, slowness, and the ordinary rhythms of daily life. Turns out, I feel freer, lighter, and downright happier when I am living a life of relative anonymity.

### Embracing the Flat-Bread Life

Around the time I slipped out the back door of social media, I read this verse in Paul's first letter to the Corinthians—words that resonated deeply with me: "So let's live our part in the Feast, not as raised bread swollen with the yeast of evil, but as flat bread—simple, genuine, unpretentious" (1 Corinthians 4:7–8). My husband sometimes bakes naan, a type of Middle Eastern flat bread, and as I read Paul's words, I could see the naan in my mind's eye: light, flat, hand-shaped rounds, slightly browned, warm from the oven and set on the rack to cool. I could taste it in my mouth: unadorned and plain yet satisfying and filling.

I knew when I read Paul's words that in the deepest part of myself, I desired a flat-bread kind of life. I yearned for a life that is simple and ordinary, yet still deeply satisfying. I was tired of trying to puff myself up on the outside, to rise to something bigger and more impressive, to be exceptional. I wanted to be filled from the inside, and knowing and understanding that about myself gave me a new sense of inner strength, power, and peace.

In his book *Run with the Horses*, Eugene Peterson observes that "any part of our lives that is given over to the crowd makes it and us worse. The larger the crowd, the smaller our lives." But, he goes on to say, "Every time we retrieve a part of our life from the crowd and respond to God's call to us, we are that much more ourselves, more human. Every time we reject the habits of the crowd and practice the disciplines of faith, we become a little more alive."[8]

Stepping away from social media and quieting my ego was one of the many ways I retrieved part of my life from the crowd during the winter of my soul. In my work as an author, I had turned over a big part of my life and myself to "the crowd"—to my "audience," to potential followers, to influencers, and to the publishing industry as a whole. The more I strove to win the affection and attention of the crowd, the smaller and more constrained my life became and the more I became a less complete and authentic person.

To be clear, "the crowd" was not the problem; I was the problem. My desire to woo the crowd was driven not only by a need to feel seen, valuable, and worthwhile, it was also driven by a desire for what the crowd—namely the influencers—could potentially offer me: more followers, more readers, more book sales and, ultimately, more recognition.

I knew if I could get the influencers to like me and value my work, they could help drive my success. I sold my soul to the crowd.

Peterson's observation is spot-on. When we give any part of ourselves to the crowd, we are the worse for it. Ultimately, the more I laser-focused my efforts on winning the favor of the crowd at all costs, the smaller and more worthless I felt as a person. Deep down, though I never would have admitted it to myself at the time, I knew exactly what I was doing: I knew I was selling my soul. My purpose was singular—to become successful and, therefore, known—and I whittled myself to a shell of a person to achieve it. It wasn't until I turned away from the crowd by exiling myself from both my profession and from the many people who—unbeknownst to them—I had allowed to take hold of my soul that I began to retrieve parts of my lost life and my lost self.

"Hiding is a way of staying alive," acknowledges David Whyte. "We live in a time of the dissected soul, the immediate disclosure; our thoughts, imaginings and longings exposed to the light too much, too early, and too often, our best qualities squeezed too soon into a world already awash with ideas that oppress our sense of self and our sense of others."[9] Like the insects and animals that camouflage themselves to survive, my withdrawal into invisibility was a means of survival. So focused was I on achieving the title and identity of "successful author," I lost sight of who I was at my core.

It took me a long time, but eventually I began to respond to God's call to turn away from idolatry—from the futile attempt to find my worth and value in external sources—and turn back to the true source of my value as a person created by God. I did not turn back with ease and grace. In fact, I went kicking and screaming. But eventually, in turning away from the crowd; withdrawing into a self-imposed exile;

and embracing quiet, invisibility, simplicity, and smallness, I began to feel my life and myself turning as well. I felt myself beginning to open into a new spaciousness, a new place from which to see.

## Quieting Outside Voices

During the months I was disconnected from social media, I read Cal Newport's book *Digital Minimalism*, which helped me figure out a plan for reentering the social media space if or when it came time for that. I knew I didn't want to fall into my old scrolling habits. I also didn't want to fall into my old habits of looking to social media for validation. I wanted social media to work for me, rather than feel like I was working for it.

The key to living successfully as a digital minimalist, according to Newport, is to "optimize" what brings you value while minimizing mindless scrolling. In other words, he says, "Take steps to extract the good from these technologies while sidestepping what is bad."[10] Aim for long-term meaning over short-term satisfaction, and "focus online time on a small number of carefully selected and optimized activities that strongly support the things you value."[11]

When it comes to social media, Instagram is my Achilles' heel. It's where I'm most likely to scroll mindlessly. It's where I go when I'm bored or to kill time in the dentist's waiting room. It's where I spend the largest portion of my social media time each day, and I knew it had the potential to derail my best "digital minimalism" intentions. On the other hand, Instagram does have the potential to add value to my life in that it offers me the opportunity to discover and "explore" the kind of natural landscapes I don't have access to it in my real life here in Nebraska. I also appreciate

Instagram as a place to connect with people I know and like but from whom I am physically distant.

I knew I didn't want to abandon it entirely, so with Newport's advice in mind, I spent many hours curating my Instagram feed so that it better reflected what I value. I unfollowed hundreds of people, keeping only those accounts in my feed that aligned with the values I identified as important to me, principally: friends and people I know in real life but don't see as often as I would like; people who live in Nebraska (friends as well as local businesses I try to support); photographers who share beautiful pictures of nature; and people I might not know in person but who share meaningful content that resonates with me.

I also unfollowed dozens of people who triggered feelings of insecurity or worthlessness in me—not because of anything particular they said or did or wrote or because of who they were as people, but because of who I was in that season in my life. These were people I admired and, in many cases, people whom I'd wanted to notice me when I was still working as an author. In the quiet of my social media hiatus, I realized that even after leaving publishing, I had still been in the habit of listening more to their voices than to the voice of my own soul. I also realized that I had spent a large part of my online life shape-shifting in an effort to attract the notice and approval of the influencers. In other words, I had spent so long trying to be like other people, I had forgotten how to be me.

It was surprisingly hard for me to unfollow these Instagram influencers. I knew many of these women (and a handful of men) personally and had met many of them in real life. I considered several of them to be acquaintances or even friends. I worried they would discover I'd unfollowed them, and I didn't want to hurt anyone's feelings. I also wrestled with the fear of missing out: *What if something big and important happens and I miss it altogether?* I knew, though, that I had to create some healthy boundaries for myself, and one way to do that was to distance myself from the online voices that made it easier for me to fall into my old bad habits.

Creating a safe space for myself online helped me disrupt the unhealthy patterns of comparison and approval- and affirmation-seeking I had established over many years of online networking and platform-building. Because I didn't know what "everyone else" was doing, I wasn't compelled to hop on the latest hashtag bandwagon or try to capitalize on the latest social media trends. And because I had unfollowed so many influencers, I no longer felt compelled to tag them in my posts, hoping to attract their notice. I became more comfortable doing my own thing on Instagram. I posted a lot of photos of trees and images of the tallgrass prairie, simply because they appealed to me. And because I was no longer trying to attract the attention of the influencers I admired, I was also less likely to shape-shift online—and, over time, was able to discover and settle into my own authentic voice.

I now understand that unfollowing people on social media—even people we know, respect, and like—is okay. In fact, it's more than okay; it's imperative for our mental and spiritual health that we decide for our own selves who we will allow to influence us and impact us, both in our online spaces and in our real-life circles. We get to decide which voices are good for us and which—maybe for this season, maybe for longer—are not. And if there are voices in our spaces that do not align with who we are or who we want to be, voices that have become too large or loud in our lives or voices that make it more difficult for us to be our best selves, we are allowed to quiet these voices in our spaces. There might come a day when we allow these voices back in; there might not. Either way, it's okay.

## Beneath the Surface

The first couple months of my self-imposed exile and social-media hiatus felt good. After ten years of sprinting on the treadmill of productivity and achievement, it was a relief to retreat into quietness and invisibility, to rest without any expectations, goals, or deadlines. As one restful month blurred into the next, however, I found myself beginning to chafe at the slower, quieter rhythms of my life. Though I knew I still needed time to catch my breath, find my equilibrium and tend to my soul in the present moment, I itched to recover faster and get on to the next thing. It felt like it was time to move on; hadn't I rested enough already?

Because we are so accustomed to moving at our culture's pace, rather than at the pace of our own soul, we are often tempted to rush through this necessary season of dormancy and rest. Society will always insist we should be making good use of our limited time. Our 24/7, productivity-oriented culture will always try to bully us into action. We might even bully our own selves, convincing ourselves that we've rested long enough, that it's time to get on to producing again. After all, how are we any value to our community, to our consumerist culture, and to humanity if we aren't actually doing or producing anything?

But here's the thing I've learned about dormancy and rest: there is much more going on below the surface than meets the eye. I didn't realize it all those years ago, but there was actually a lot happening in my neighbors' burlap-wrapped rose bushes and beneath the dirt in which they were rooted. The rose canes, buried in leaves and mulch, were dormant, but under the frozen soil, the roses' roots were still very much alive, steadily being nourished by the carbohydrates and sugars the plant had transported down from its leaves at the end of the growing season. The roses were "actively waning"—surviving off stored nutrients, biding their time and conserving their energy until longer days and warmer temperatures signaled it was time to begin growing again. All the while, even in their dormancy, quiet but important work and growth was taking place deep in their roots.

As I mentioned earlier, roses that awaken from dormancy too soon to begin preparations for growing and blooming can be damaged or even killed by a sudden freeze. Completing a full cycle of dormancy is as important for a rose bush's long-term health as proper fertilizing, watering, and pruning are during the growing season.

Likewise, seasons of retreat and rest are a critical part of our long-term physical, mental, creative, and spiritual health. Only we and God can know and determine the appropriate duration of our fallow season. Our dormancy might last just a few weeks. It might last a few months. It might, as in my case, last a few years. At the time I am typing this sentence, more than two years have passed since I signed the Termination of Contract paperwork and stepped out of the publishing arena. During much of this time I have been "actively waning"—learning who I am, uncovering my authentic voice, growing more fully into myself.

When we find ourselves feeling pressured to produce before we are ready, we can gently remind ourselves that we need not constantly hustle, push, and strive. We remember that even in stillness, even when all our outward motion and effort come to a standstill, God declares us worthy. His promise to us—a promise we receive and trust in faith— is that he is always moving on our behalf. Let us take our cue from my neighbors' rose bushes, wrapped in burlap and resting for the winter. Let us remember that God is present and at work in us even in, *especially in*, our cessation.

Though society insists there's no need and no time for rest, God tells us a different story through his creation. In the winter of our soul, when it looks like absolutely nothing at all is happening, God is indeed still creating us anew. Let us receive his gift.

# CHAPTER SIX

# Stella the Cat

*The senses don't just make sense of life in
bold or subtle acts of clarity, they tear reality
apart into vibrant morsels and reassemble
them into a meaningful pattern.*

DIANE ACKERMAN

Sitting in a sunny spot in my front yard on an unseasonably
warm afternoon in February, my eyes closed, my face tipped
toward the barely warm sun, I hear the birds—an indistin-
guishable cacophony of twitters and cackles from the trees,
the roof, the power lines. I listen as the blur of chatter begins
to separate into distinct calls. The screech of a blue jay. The
staccato tap of a nuthatch on a tree trunk. The scuffle of
sparrows in the gutter. More sounds announce themselves
as I continue to sit with my eyes closed. A whisper of wind
in the white pines. My neighbor's American flag snapping in
the wind. The thrum of bass from a nearby car. A skitter of
dry leaves cartwheeling across the concrete.

The longer I pause to listen, the more I hear.

Walking with Josie later in the week, I stop to gaze up
at an enormous sycamore tree, its smooth trunk a mottled
blend of grays and greens, like military camouflage, its bare
branches strung with hundreds of seed balls dangling like
Christmas ornaments. I pick one up from the ground and
carry it home. Later, sitting at my desk, I hold the seed ball

in my palm, and I see that it's made of hundreds of individual seeds, each shaped like a tiny railroad spike with a wisp of fluff on the end, its magic carpet come spring.

Standing in my sunroom on a frigid morning, I press my forehead to the cold glass and gaze out into the backyard. There are buds on the magnolia tree. I can see the fuzzed sepals still tightly clasped, and I imagine white petals drowsing inside, wrapped in a smooth blanket of warmth, biding their time for the remaining weeks of winter before opening to the spring sun.

On another of our daily walks, I stand with Josie at the edge of a snow-dusted field. She strains the leash taut as we both watch a young fox play in the late-afternoon stillness. His russet coat catches the sun's last glow as he picks up a honey locust seed pod in his teeth, tosses his sleek head back, and flings the pod into the air—leaping and then pouncing on it when it lands in the snow, agile and exuberant as he practices his predatory skills. It's such a simple thing, but in that instant, as the young fox cavorts in the waning sunlight, time slows. Everything but that very moment falls away as the Spirit moves across the surface of the day, beckoning with an invitation to come closer, to look, to listen.

The more I slow to look, the more I see.

During the winter of my soul, as I intentionally quieted my environment and myself, my body and mind began to feel more grounded. For months my brain had felt like it was a bunch of balloons bumping along with the unpredictable currents, my thoughts apt to float away at any moment. Now, in the stillness, my mind felt more tethered. I felt more aware, more present. My senses were sharper. Being grounded in my own body, in my own place, in my actual real life began to give rise to a keen attentiveness.

## A Sensory Avenue into Our Soul

For most humans, sight is our dominant sense—researchers estimate we receive up to 80 percent of incoming information through sight. Yet as the late poet philosopher John O'Donohue observed, "Many of us have made our world so familiar that we do not see it anymore." O'Donohue challenges us to ask ourselves before we close our eyes each night, "What did I really see this day?" He suggests we might be surprised by how little we recall.[1]

I know this has often been the case for me. I mindlessly tumble through my day on autopilot without ever really seeing or noticing anything. I spend a lot of time in my own head, planning for the future, rehashing what has already past. I am always somewhere other than right here. Decreasing some of the extra stimulation and input that typically comes from my immersion in social and traditional media helped create space for a deeper focus and attentiveness to flourish, which in turn began to open the way to a new spaciousness in my body, mind, and soul.

"It is a startling truth that how you see and what you see determine how and who you will be," O'Donohue writes.[2] This truth has been borne out time and time again in my own life. Cluttering my vision with an endless stream of images pouring from the tiny rectangle of my phone makes for a stifled, narrow view of life and, subsequently, contributes to a stifled, narrow view of myself. On the other hand, opening my eyes and ears to details in my everyday surroundings—the enormous variety of bird calls in my own backyard, the intricacy of a sycamore seed ball, a clasped magnolia bud, a young fox's sleek russet coat glowing in the sun—is a much-needed reminder of the infinite vastness of the world around me . . . and the infinite vastness contained within me.

Sight and sound are the most accessible senses for many of us, but our other senses can serve as a way into a deeper part of ourselves as well. During a weekend trip to visit my friend Sarah in Tennessee, I spent hours reclined on her sofa with a weighted blanket tucked around my legs and her orange tabby, Stella, settled into my lap. Stella loved to be petted, and I was happy to oblige. Stroking her soft fur and feeling the vibrations of her rhythmic purring reverberating under my hand was restful and grounding in a way that was both unfamiliar and yet deeply soothing.

I was surprised to recognize that I needed this comfort. I realized I had been longing for it without even recognizing what that longing was. Petting Stella revealed a new, untapped part of myself that I had neglected and perhaps even intentionally ignored.

Sometimes the simple act of opening ourselves to new or unfamiliar sensory experiences in our bodies can show us where we have neglected ourselves or where we are in need. As O'Donohue observes in *Anam Cara*, "Your senses link you intimately with the divine within you and around you. Attunement to the senses can warm and heal the atrophied feelings that are barriers exiling us from ourselves and separating us from each other."[3]

Feeling Stella's soft fur under my palm, feeling the weight of the blanket and her body on my lap, witnessing her trust in me and observing her ability to rest helped me see that I not only desire comfort and rest, but also that I long to feel secure and safe. Over my lifetime I've built self-protective barriers around myself that I thought were necessary but which, over the long term, have prevented me from opening to and allowing myself to feel this deep need. I thought I was protecting myself from vulnerability, but, as O'Donohue acknowledges, in reality I was distancing myself from my true self and from others. As silly or strange as it might

sound, petting Stella and allowing myself to sink deeply into
the experience of touch and groundedness was an unexpected bridge into my own emotions and my own needs.


*A Pathway into Our Emotions . . . and Ourselves*

Science supports this link between the senses and our emotions. Research has shown that smell, for instance, is the
sense most closely linked to the hippocampus—the part
of the brain that's connected to our memories—as well as
to the limbic system, the emotional center of the brain.[4]
If you've even gotten a whiff of a scent that unexpectedly
evoked a powerful memory and a strong emotion, seemingly
out of nowhere, you know this is true.

I recall a time many years ago when I was enveloped in the
scent of perfume wafting in the wake of an elderly woman
walking across the grocery store parking lot. I recognized the
fragrance immediately as Chanel No. 5, my grandmother's
signature scent, and as it rolled over me like a gentle wave, I
was instantly transported back three decades to my grandparents' house. In that moment, standing motionless in the
grocery store parking lot, I experienced an immediate sense
of peace, love, and security, along with a surprising feeling
of yearning rising up in me. In that moment, I remembered
and felt in the deepest part of myself the delight, comfort,
safety, and unconditional love that I had known and experienced as a child with my grandmother.

Those memories and that feeling of love and security are
precious to me, and yet, as I have matured into an adult, I
have not acknowledged that I need and long for that kind of
comfort, nurturing, and sense of safety. I have not sought it
because, honestly, I think I have been afraid of being disappointed. I've questioned whether that kind of comfort and

security is tenable as an adult, so I have not given myself permission to desire it or seek it. I have kept myself at arm's length from my own longing, and yet, this longing is an integral part of who I am.

For those of us disconnected from our emotions and our own longings, paying attention to what our senses are telling us can serve as a helpful pathway not only toward identifying and feeling our emotions and longings, but also toward understanding who we are in the deepest part of ourselves. "The senses are generous pathways that can bring you home," says O'Donohue. "By being attuned to the wisdom of your senses, you will never become an exile in your own life, an outsider lost in an external spiritual place that your will and intellect have constructed."[5]

Recently, as I was experimenting with a guided meditation, I experienced the sensation of floating in a warm pool. I saw in my mind's eye the clear water lapping at the pool's edge, the sunlight glinting off the surface. I felt my hair fanning out behind my head, the softness of the warm water beneath my fingertips, the cool air on my forehead and cheeks.

In that moment I recalled an early morning visit to the hot springs pool at Glenwood Springs on a family trip to Colorado several summers ago. My husband, our sons, and I were the only people in the pool that morning, and I remember lying back in the water just as the sun began to spill over the surrounding hills. Propping my heels on the edge of the pool to keep myself from drifting, I floated, arms spread wide, eyes closed, the noises around me muffled by the water covering my ears. I remember feeling a sense of complete peace, a lightness in my body and my spirit, a blissful emptiness in my mind as I surrendered to the sensation of being held.

It was, I realize now, an experience reminiscent of the safety and comfort of the womb. Years later when I returned to that sensation during the guided meditation, I understood that I was opening myself to a deeply buried longing. I needed to be held and comforted. I needed to know I was safe and secure. And, even more important, I needed to let myself need this comfort, nurturing, and security—to dismantle the long-standing walls I had erected and allow myself to be vulnerable, soft, and tender.

Each of us has deep needs and longings, but for many of us, these needs and longings have been hidden for a long time. During the winter of my soul, as I began to pay closer attention to the sights, sounds, smells, and touch that stirred me, I began to connect with my emotions for the first time in many years. Rather than turning away, burying, or fearing these emotions, I began instead to turn toward them, and as a result, I found myself turning more intimately and authentically toward God.

In the deepest part of ourselves, we want to know that we can trust God to receive, accept, and embrace our whole selves. If you're like me, you might understand intellectually that this kind of trust is possible but, at the same time, struggle to know and believe it in your heart and soul. This is where our senses can help, offering an entryway into a deeper knowing of and relationship with God.

As Kathleen Norris writes, "We have reached the limits of our knowing and are dependent on our senses to 'know' for us."[6] Experiencing God's love, comfort, safety, and presence through our senses, rather than merely through our intellectual understanding, can open a new way into vulnerability and authenticity and, ultimately, into God's presence.

# CHAPTER SEVEN

# Greenhouse Philodendron

*We must listen to what is supporting us. We must
listen to what is encouraging us. We must listen to
what is urging us. We must listen to what is alive in us.*

RICHARD ROHR

Most plants love the sun, but I have one in particular—a spider plant—that seems to crave it more than the others. It leans, reaching its leaves toward the light that glows bright from the sunroom windows. Every couple of weeks or so I turn its pot, forcing it to shift direction so it won't grow too lopsided. And then I wait and watch, knowing it will inevitably begin to lean toward the sun again.

This sun-loving spider plant reminds me of a sermon I once heard when I was visiting a Unitarian church in Tennessee. I don't recall the exact theme of the minister's message that morning, but I do remember that she asked us if we might begin to practice leaning toward what we love, rather than running away or trying to escape from what is hard or unpleasant.

I realized in that moment that my default mode is to flee from what is painful rather than to lean toward what might bring me comfort, healing, joy, or peace. My running takes a variety of forms. Sometimes I run by numbing myself with social media or by cleaning or shopping. Sometimes I run by performing—by trying to be the person I think I am expected to be and striving to earn approval and recognition. Sometimes I run by cramming my schedule chock-full of busyness.

None of these nor the innumerable other avoidance or numbing strategies we employ to deal with anxiety, discomfort, or unrest are particularly effective. They might ease our stress in the moment or allow us to avoid, temporarily, whatever is threatening, but in the end, they are not healthy ways to address the source of discomfort. Nor will they lead to real growth.

But what if instead, as the Unitarian pastor asked, we practiced leaning toward what we love? What if we spent more of our energy moving toward what gives us life? Might leaning toward what we love nourish and sustain us in ways that could ultimately have the potential to open a door to lasting change and deep transformation?

The winter of our soul is a time of rest, retreat, and hibernation, but it can also be a time of rich discovery, a season in which we have the time and space to explore the landscape of ourselves—our *terra incognita*—and begin to uncover the full scope of the person God created in us.

As I gave myself permission to be curious and to explore, I began to uncover previously uncharted facets of myself. It might sound strange, but this exploration of my own self took deliberate intention and work. As I mentioned in a previous chapter, I had allowed the vine—my work and my desire for success—to define me for so long, and I had put so much of my time and energy into maintaining it and feeding it, I'd overlooked the many other aspects of myself that made me uniquely me. I'd forgotten who I was. I didn't know what I enjoyed, what gave me pleasure, or even really how to have fun. I struggled to lean toward what I loved, because I didn't know what I loved.

## *Learning to Lean toward What We Love*

"Do you think it's too late for me to learn how to have fun?" I asked Brad one morning. "That's a really un-fun question to ask!" he replied, which made me laugh. But I was serious. I really wanted to know: Was it possible for responsible, rule-following, work-driven me to learn how to let go a little bit and have fun? Or was it too late—was I simply destined to be a dutiful, responsible, productive, but largely un-fun person?

Just a few days before that conversation with Brad, my son Rowan and I had driven to the sprawling Lancaster Event Center to attend the Lincoln City Library's annual used book sale. I'd marked the sale on our family calendar months before, and Rowan and I had been anticipating it for weeks, eager to see what literary treasures we would uncover among the thousands of books available at garage-sale prices. As we wound our way through the packed parking lot toward the building, recyclable grocery bags tucked under our arms, I cautioned Rowan not to get his hopes up. "The sale started two days ago, so the books are probably pretty picked over by now," I reminded him. "I don't know if there'll be anything good left." I continued along in this vein for a few more minutes until Rowan interrupted me. "You really know how to suck the fun out of everything, don't you?" he huffed. "You're like a fun vacuum."

I stopped walking. "Wait, what? What are you even talking about?" I said, genuinely flabbergasted. "I'm fun! I love fun! I'm way more fun than Dad! [When in doubt, always throw the other parent under the bus, right?] I do not 'suck the fun' out of everything! I am not a 'fun vacuum'! Why would you even say that?" Rowan shrugged and kept walking, clearly unconvinced.

In the end, we did have fun, and Rowan and I each left the library sale that morning with a hefty bag full of books. Weeks later, however, I was still thinking about his accusation. *Do I suck the fun out of everything?* I wondered. I was reminded of the classic Dr. Seuss book, *The Cat in the Hat.* Was I the nail-biting, naysaying, fretting fish alongside the exuberant, fun-loving, Cat-in-the-Hat Rowan? (Rowan, it should be said, is a seven on the Enneagram—also known as The Enthusiast. An Enneagram three gave birth to an Enneagram seven. God laughs.) *Do I even know how to have fun?* I wondered if perhaps I'd camped out a bit too long (read: my whole life) in the realm of responsibility, rule-following, and routine at the expense of spontaneity, creativity, and fun.

Being responsible and fulfilling obligations are very good habits, to be sure. But I'm beginning to realize that "being responsible" can also be a cleverly disguised means of self-protection. Keeping on task, meeting deadlines, and ticking items off a never-ending to-do list are all ways I attempt to maintain control over my life. After all, if I'm in control, nothing bad can happen, right? While I know this equation is deeply flawed, I still often live like it's the truth.

The same can be said for my tendency to manage expectations. Entering into an experience with rock-bottom expectations is one of the ways I try to protect myself (and those I love) from disappointment. The trouble with this attempt at self-protection, though, is that not only is it not fail-safe, it can also detract from and dilute the experience itself (in other words, as Rowan so succinctly stated, it can "suck the fun out of everything").

One of the things I did during the winter of my soul was to work through a goal-planner (an exercise, I realize, that sounds very un-fun, but stay with me here) that prompted me to consider who I am and who I might want to become.

As a result of that self-reflection, I identified six goals for myself—one of which was to have more fun in the upcoming year. It feels ridiculous to admit that, and it felt ridiculous to pen it into my planner as an actual goal. It seemed frivolous and more than a little silly. I mean, *this* is my big issue . . . to have more fun? Woe is me, right?

And yet, while I know it is an extraordinary privilege to have the means to focus on fun, I also believe that having fun is important because it's one of the ways we live most fully as God intended. I believe God created us to be responsible and productive, but I also believe he created us to be playful, creative, and fun-loving—full of, as the French say, "joie de vivre," the joy of living. Having fun is one of the many ways we come alive. Having fun is one of the ways we lean toward what we love. I don't want to ditch my responsible, dutiful, rule-following nature entirely, but I do want to embrace a more open, curious, creative, whole way of living, which means nurturing and growing the parts of myself that have lain dormant for decades or perhaps are still yet to be discovered.

I didn't know what to do with myself once the vine was eliminated. I had to relearn—and in some cases, learn for the first time—how to lean toward what I loved. It wasn't enough, I now understood, simply to turn away from that which was harmful and unhealthy. It also wasn't enough to settle comfortably into my default mode of responsibility, duty, structure, and rule-following. That space, I was coming to understand, was too small for me.

I had lived most of my life trying to meet the expectations—real and perceived—of others. As a result, I found, at nearly fifty years old, that I had no idea what I wanted or what I loved. It was high time I identified those practices, habits, and activities that were healthy, restorative, enlivening, and fun. It was time for me to figure out what made me come alive and lean toward it with a spirit of curiosity and exploration. It was time to step out of my small, safe space of structure, rules, and responsibility and into the wider, undefined space of the unknown.

"Leave room for the encounters that will change us in ways we can't yet see," writes Jenny Odell. "Acknowledge we are each a confluence of forces that exceed our own understanding."[1] Honestly, when I first read Odell's words, I found them scary. I don't like to think of myself as "confluence of forces" that I can't control or understand. I don't want to "leave room for encounters" I can't predict or see coming, because that feels risky. And yet, at the same time, I also heard possibility and potential in Odell's words that ignited an unfamiliar excitement in me. I was intrigued, curious. I wanted to explore the unfamiliar practice of leaning toward what I loved. And so I cautiously stepped into a season of trying new things.

### Our Habits Can Inhibit Us

One of the first things I did in my season of trying new things was to join a gym for the first time in my life. For decades I had declared often and to whomever would listen that I was "not a gym person." I was a runner who ran outdoors, I told myself (and others). And that was true.

As an outdoor runner, I relished the bite of winter on my cheeks in January and the heaviness of summer's humidity pressing against my limbs and surging thick into my lungs in June. I loved to glimpse what was happening in the landscape as I ran past—from the first hardy crocus pushing through the snow in early spring to the last of the goldenrod and purple aster fading to dust in late fall. Running outdoors enlivened and energized me, and for many years it was my exercise of choice. In fact, for many years, running outdoors (or occasionally, if the weather was truly horrifying, on our basement treadmill) was my only form of exercise.

Until, that is, my running habit was sidelined by a chronic injury. Restless and agitated without my regular cardio, I was finally compelled to accompany Brad to the Y to give the elliptical machine a reluctant try. Much to my surprise, I discovered I enjoyed it—not so much the elliptical (which is frightfully boring), but rather, the whole gym "experience."

I found I embraced the camaraderie of exercising silently side-by-side with strangers before the sun has yet to peek over the horizon. I relished the feel of the smooth vinyl under my body as I stretched on the blue mat and caught my breath after finishing my workout. Watching people of every shape, age, and size running, walking, pushing, pulling, lifting, climbing, and spinning inspired and motivated me. There was an unspoken sense of community among the pre-dawn gym exercisers. We were a club of sorts, and I felt like I belonged. Turns out, after all these years of resisting it and denying it, I am "a gym person" after all.

I am a creature of habit. This explains why I have run—at least until I got injured—the exact same route three to four times a week for the past eighteen years. It explains why I have eaten the same midmorning snack (sixteen almonds) at the same time (10:00 a.m.) every day for the past ten years. It explains why I read for at least a half hour every night before I go to sleep, a habit I've had for as long as I can remember.

I could give you a dozen such examples. Routines and habits are comforting because they are familiar. They also offer us a sense of safety, security, and structure, and, because they eliminate the decision-making process, our routines and habits can help us be more productive and efficient; we can focus our mental energy on what matters. I don't stand in front of my open kitchen cabinet every morning at 10:00

a.m. debating over what I'll choose for my midmorning snack. I already know: sixteen almonds. I count the nuts into a bowl and move on to the more pressing tasks at hand.

On the other hand, I'm also learning that this kind of structured living can, over time, inhibit growth and lead to stagnation. "Those who attempt to work too long with a formula, even their own formula, eventually leach themselves of their creative truths," writes Julia Cameron in *The Artist's Way*.[2] Cameron is referring specifically to the creative process, but we can say the same about our own selves. A formula can be helpful. Routines and habits can help us stay focused and meet our goals. But if we become enslaved to it, a formula can also hem us in and inhibit our growth.

Ultimately, being too wedded to our routines and habits—to our "formula," as Cameron calls it—will suffocate our soul. In limiting our self-identity (e.g. "I am not a gym person"), we limit our potential to expand into a fuller, more complete version of ourselves. A season of self-imposed hibernation, retreat, and rest can offer an opportunity to break our former default patterns of being in order to begin to set new ways of being in place. It can be a time to till our hardened, stale soil—to turn over our old ways and bring a new, fresh way of living to the surface.

"You can spend years lost in the wilderness of your own mechanical, spiritual programs. You can perish in a famine of your own making," John O'Donohue acknowledges. "If you work with a different rhythm, you will come easily and naturally home to yourself. . . . If you attend to yourself and seek to come into your presence, you will find exactly the right rhythm for your own life."[3] I spent years—my entire adult life, actually—lost in the wilderness of my own programs. Ultimately, as O'Donohue says, I perished in a famine of my own making. I thought quitting my job was the end of something; turns out, it was merely the beginning of a long season of uncovering and living into a completely different rhythm.

### We Contain Multitudes

One of the things I learned during my season of trying new things is that growth and transformation don't always look or feel very dramatic. Sometimes the process of growing more fully into our true selves is born out of a series of small, seemingly disconnected decisions and steps that slowly, over time, begin to broaden our understanding of who we are. This might sound strange, but buying a houseplant was one such step for me.

One afternoon while my son Noah and I were exploring a new-to-us local greenhouse, wending our way between stately candelabra cactus and lush fiddle leaf figs, I felt the inexplicable urge to buy a plant. I have a handful of house-plants—mostly succulents because they still thrive when neglected—scattered in various spots around my sunroom, but I've never considered myself "a plant person." Suddenly, though, immersed in all that fecundity, breathing in the rich, humid scent of new growth, I knew something new about myself. The realization was like the clear, sharp chime of a church bell reverberating across an Italian piazza: Plants make me happy! I want my home to be filled with lots of different plants!

I initially resisted the desire to buy a plant that day in the greenhouse. I'm not kidding when I tell you it was a fif-teen-minute epic battle to get myself to buy a $20 philoden-dron. For starters, my practical, responsible self was making a very sound argument against the purchase. *You don't need a plant,* my responsible self insisted. *Don't spend money on something you'll probably kill anyway. This is dumb.* Buying a plant for no good reason seemed frivolous, perhaps even irresponsible—a waste of money. I tried to reason my way away from the unexpected curiosity and longing I felt bubbling up inside me. After examining several of the plants, I walked away.

A few minutes later, however, I found myself back at the philodendrons. Something deep inside me knew it was important to pay attention to and answer this unexpected, unfamiliar desire. In that moment, I knew I needed to follow a longing that had absolutely nothing to do with outcomes or goals or achievements. This, I realized, was what it felt like to discover and lean toward what I loved.

I bought a philodendron and a white pot that day, transplanted it on the driveway when I got home, and placed it on top of a bookcase near my desk in the sunroom. I fuss over this plant (and the many others I have purchased since then; I have indeed become "a plant lady") like it's a newborn baby, spritzing it with water, gently rubbing a soft dust cloth over its leaves, turning the pot a half-inch this way, a half-inch that way, carrying it out to the back patio on sunny days so it can bask in the bright light. Months after buying it, every time I look at the philodendron on my bookshelf, I feel a deep satisfaction and joy.

It's important to pay attention to these awakenings, to these tiny pricks of self-knowledge and self-discovery, even when they seem small or silly or strange, because they can help us uncover a fuller sense of ourselves. Recognizing my desire to buy a plant that day in the greenhouse was like answering a quiet knock on the door of my own soul. Opening that door didn't transform my whole life. It didn't remake me into a new person. But it told me something new about myself, something that helped me recognize that I was more, much more, than who I'd always assumed I was.

It was exciting to realize that there were facets of me that, until that point, I had never explored or even acknowledged before.

"There's something enlivening about expanding our self-definition," acknowledges Cameron, "and a risk does exactly that."[4] True, going to the gym or buying a houseplant are hardly risky endeavors, but at the same time, I believe there is something important and telling even in these small steps. Any step outside the boundaries by which we have defined and contained ourselves is a step into newness, and stepping into newness, no matter how seemingly small or inconsequential, is always a risk. But it's in these smallest of steps and these smallest of risks that we begin to recognize and embrace the many facets of ourselves. When we allow ourselves to open to these small moments of knowing and lean toward them, we unclasp something deep within us, which in turn opens the way to living more fully and wholly as our true selves.

Until I gave myself the opportunity to explore a new way to exercise, I didn't know that I could enjoy working out at the gym and that there was a whole undiscovered community there. Until I gave myself permission to say yes to a seemingly silly desire, I didn't know that being surrounded by and caring for plants brings me joy and peace. Working out at a gym with other people energizes and motivates me. Having plants in my home enlivens me, fulfills a deep-seated need to nurture life and brings me a satisfaction that is free from expectations or outcomes. I was nearly fifty years old when I discovered these new aspects of myself, and it thrills me to my core to realize there are undoubtedly many more facets yet to be uncovered.

"I am large, I contain multitudes," the poet Walt Whitman wrote.[5] Our depths are fathomless; we are each more than we can ever possibly imagine. I believe God created this depth, this largeness in us as a reflection of him, and I believe he gifted each one of us with these multitudes within us so that we can experience the full breadth and depth of his love. When we pay attention to our longings, when we answer the knock at the door of our own soul and begin to lean toward what we love, we open into an expansiveness and a spaciousness we never even knew was there. Like the spider plant on my bookshelf leaning toward the sunlight, we lean into the fullest experience of ourselves, coming closer to the God who created us and sustains us in love.

# CHAPTER EIGHT

# Tulip Bulbs

*Winter is a womb in which to grow.*

GUNILLA NORRIS

In October of 2010, one month after my mother-in-law's death, my boys—who were nine and five at the time—and I decided to plant a tulip garden in her memory. We drove to the local nursery and stood in front of the bins, carefully studying the placards posted on each one, deciding on our desired color scheme as the hothouse plastic snapped and flapped in the late autumn wind. After much deliberation, we filled four white paper bags with bulbs in the perfect shades—plum, yellow, scarlet, and orange—aiming for a symphony of raucous color come spring.

Back home, we intentionally chose to plant our memorial garden in the far back corner of the yard, where we would be able to see it from every window facing the backyard. I imagined standing at the kitchen window come spring, gazing out at an orderly display of flowers, concentric circles of colors ringing the box like a proper English garden. That vision was quickly shattered when Rowan unceremoniously dumped the contents of all four bags into a single mixed-up mound of bulbs in the dirt. It was just as well, and in a way perfectly fitting for my mother-in-law's memorial garden. Janice had never been distracted by perfectionism. She would have much preferred Rowan's enthusiasm and eagerness over a meticulously laid out, color-coded formal garden any day.

And so, as elm leaves swirled to the ground around us that late October afternoon, the boys and I got to work. We dug hole after hole in the dry, crumbling dirt, settling each bulb snugly into its tomb. Trowels clanking, we swished the soil over their papery skins, patted the dirt smooth, and then sat back on our heels to survey the bed, satisfied with our work.

All winter that year I watched from the window over the kitchen sink, the eight panes steaming from the hot water, my hands in warm suds as snow blanketed the garden. The bulbs slept beneath slush and snow and frozen dirt as I scoured fry pans, rinsed juice glasses, and brushed crumbs from the countertops into my cupped palm. Winter felt long and dark as we grieved the loss of Janice.

When the weather finally began to warm in March, the boys and I began each day with a trip out to the garden. Throughout that dreary early spring, we pulled on our boots and ventured outside to bend low over the raised bed in the back corner. Hands on our knees, we peered at the dirt, hoping for a glimpse of anything that might signal that something was actually happening underground.

Finally one warmish morning we spotted fissures slicing jagged through the soil. A few days later the first tender shoots surprised us with their hue, not green at all, but tinted pink, like delicate, pointed tongues tentatively reaching out of the cracked earth, eager for a lick of the warm sun. Over the following weeks the shoots sprung from the softening ground, unfurling leaves, then stems, then buds, until finally the tulips burst into a chorus of brilliant color even I hadn't quite expected.

Janice's memorial garden turned out better—more beautiful, more lush, and more vibrant—than we had ever imagined was possible the day we buried the bulbs in the soil. All winter long the bulbs had lain quiet under the cold dirt until it was time for them to sprout and grow and bloom. It seemed a miracle that those papery husks we'd dropped into dry holes and covered with crumbling soil on a bleak autumn day had become, with no help from us at all, something so new and bright and beautiful.

One of the many important truths I learned during the long winter of my soul is that God's kingdom here on earth flourishes—and we flourish in God's kingdom—not because of what *we* do but because of what *God* does. "The Kingdom of God is like a farmer who scatters seed on the ground," Jesus reminds us. "Night and day, *while he is asleep* or awake, the seed sprouts and grows, but he does not understand how it happens" (Mark 4:26–28 NLT, emphasis added). As someone who has lived the try-hard life for most of my days, these words give me great peace. We shouldn't become complacent, refusing to participate in our own growth and transformation or neglecting to do our part to bear fruit in the world, but we can trust that God's transformative work is happening within us even when we are asleep to it.

Like the tulip bulbs quietly percolating under winter's cold soil, God's work in us begins before we are even aware of it and continues in us even when we cannot yet see the results. In fact, God's work in us was begun before the beginning of time. Often, we do not even understand how this growth happens, but we trust God to see it through.

## Dropping Our Nets

"Come," Jesus said to four fishermen who were busily preparing and casting their nets into the lake, "follow me, and I will show you how to fish for people" (Matthew 4:19 NLT).

In his Gospel, Matthew reports that upon hearing Jesus'
call, Peter and Andrew—and a few minutes later, James and
John—immediately dropped their nets, left their boats and
all their fishing equipment, and followed Jesus. They left
their livelihood as fishermen. They left what was familiar
and comfortable, what was known, to follow Jesus into the
unknown.

When I read this story recently I heard a question
reverberate in my soul. *What,* my soul asked, *might Jesus
be asking you to drop and leave behind in order to follow
him?* I admit, my initial answer was, "Nothing." After all, I
reasoned, I had already dropped my proverbial nets; I had
already left everything behind. I'd quit book publishing.
I'd left my career and calling. I'd quit writing my monthly
column for the local newspaper. I'd quit speaking. I'd closed
down my professional social media accounts and stepped
away from the work of building a platform. I'd relinquished
the familiar. I'd let go of what I knew. Surely, I assumed,
there couldn't be more to drop, right? Turns out, there was.

In his book *The Wisdom Pattern*, Richard Rohr identi-
fies seven ways of "knowing reality": intellectual knowing,
volitional knowing, emotional knowing, bodily or sensory
knowing, imaginal knowing, aesthetic knowing, and epiph-
anic knowing. He explains that by "ways of knowing," he
means the ways "we come to see what we see"[1]—in other
words, the lenses through which we view ourselves, our
world, and God.[2] None of these ways of knowing is necessarily better than another; rather, each of the seven ways of
knowing is an important step on the journey toward a better
understanding of our true selves.

Reading *The Wisdom Pattern* and exploring the seven
ways of knowing has helped me understand that I feel most
comfortable and confident in the realm of intellectual knowing. Many of us in the Western world, especially those of us

who have benefitted from the privilege of higher education, have been taught to value rational scientific thought and knowledge and information acquisition. While I have begun to explore some of the other ways of knowing during the last year, my sweet spot is still intellectual knowing. I like to learn. I love research. I underline sentences, dog-ear pages, and take notes on virtually everything I read, including fiction. I'm a "head" person. Nothing makes me happier than gathering facts, evidence, knowledge, and answers—especially, it turns out, when my research topic is my own self.

In addition to the Year of Quitting Everything, 2019 was also a season of deep soul-searching for me. I read several spiritual and secular "self-help" books, reentered counseling, and filled journal after journal with questions and reflections. I was on a quest, a pilgrimage of sorts, to uncover my true, God-created self, and I was determined to leave no stone unturned. I dove into my year of self-discovery with gusto, and as a result, it was an exhilarating, gratifying, transformational season.

As time went on, however, God also began to show me something important about my desire for knowledge, information, clarity, and answers. I began to see that endless reading and research—relying on intellectual knowing—is yet another way I keep myself at arm's length from my deepest self, from others, and from God.

There's nothing wrong with turning to self-help books, experts, and gurus for guidance and insights. Many offer a tremendous depth of wisdom and compassion, and I learned a lot from what I read during my year of self-discovery. The problem arises, however, when this quest for knowledge and insight begins to supplant the deeper work. Research and reading can become an avoidance tactic. As long as we are looking for the answer "out there," we don't have to sit with what's right here in the deepest part of ourselves. As long as we assure ourselves that we are "doing the work" and are taking responsibility for our own inner transformation, we don't have to yield to God in us. Turns out, the real work is not "work" in the way we typically think of it. The real work—even the work of self-discovery—is not in doing, it's in being. Our work is not work in the way we typically think of it; our work is to surrender and receive.

### Worthy to Receive

One evening, a few months after I'd entered into this spiritual wintering period, I was sitting in my church's parking lot, waiting for Rowan to emerge from confirmation class, when a long-lost prayer from my Catholic days rose unbidden from my soul: "Lord, I am not worthy to receive you, but only say the word and I shall be healed" (the prayer was rewritten in 2011, along with other changes to the Catholic liturgy, to read: "Lord, I am not worthy that you should enter under my roof, but only say the word and my soul shall be healed."). As a child I had recited these words dutifully each week during Mass before receiving Communion, but that evening, sitting in my car and feeling the words rise up in me as the sun set over the wide plains, it was as if I was hearing them for the very first time.

The prayer comes from a story included in both the Gospels of Matthew and Luke (Matthew 8:5–13; Luke 7:1–10), in which a Roman centurion approaches Jesus to request that Jesus heal his paralyzed servant. When Jesus offers to come to the man's home, the centurion humbly declines, noting, "I do not deserve to have you come under my roof, but just say the word, and my servant will be healed" (Matthew 8:8 NIV). In other words, the centurion didn't believe he was worthy enough for Jesus to enter his home, but at the same time, he believed in Jesus' power and authority to heal his servant, even from a distance. It was a statement of both deep humility and deep faith.

As a kid, I focused much more on the first half of the centurion's prayer than the second. *Lord, I am not worthy to receive you.* I did not feel worthy to receive God—to be in God's presence. In fact, no matter what I did, how much or how hard I prayed or how "good" I was, I always felt it still wasn't enough to make me worthy for God. I never considered the second half of the prayer: that I would be made worthy by God himself—through no effort of my own, but through him in me. That evening in my church's parking lot, as I remembered the words I had recited week after week and year after year in Catholic Mass, I recalled both halves of the prayer. God reminded me that I *am* worthy to receive him and to be in his presence, not because of what I do or accomplish, or because of how "good" I am, but because God himself deems me worthy. Worthiness is *his* gift, a gift he invites us to receive.

We are healed and restored when we receive the gift of our worthiness in the manner of the centurion—with humility and faith. We trust that God is always moving on our behalf, even, like the centurion, when we can't see that movement taking place. The trouble for some of us is that we resist God's invitation to receive him. And the reason we resist is because in order to receive God, we must, like the centurion, assume a posture of openness, trust, surrender, and humility—which means we must also assume a posture of vulnerability. To receive a guest in our home is to open our home and ourselves to another, which can make us feel vulnerable. To receive God is to open our home—ourselves—to him as we are. This can make us feel vulnerable too.

"Here I am, standing right before you, and you aren't willing to receive from me the life you say you want," Jesus declared to his followers in the Gospel of John (John 5:40). Why are we not willing to receive from God the life we say we want? Why do we resist his invitation to come closer to him? Because in order to receive from Christ the life we say we want, we first need to release our clutch on the life we have—the one we cling to but is not the source of our true life. To receive we must first release this false life. Releasing opens the way to trust.

I know I tend to look to the bestselling self-help book or the spiritual guru of the hour with the hope that maybe this time, *this* one will finally provide me with The Answer. Honestly, I'm not even sure what Answer I'm looking for; nonetheless, I keep searching. When I heard Jesus ask me if I had another net to drop, I realized he was asking me to drop what had become my safety nets: my relentless doing and my reliance on intellectual knowing.

It's easier and much less scary to look outward for guidance and direction than it is to turn inward and sit quietly with God and our own selves. It's much, much easier to do than to be. It's much easier to take action than to receive. We study and research, we listen and read, we look for the quick fix in the pages of the latest bestselling book or in the advice of the most popular podcasters, but the real truth is not found there. The real truth is found in the silence and space of our own souls—and it doesn't always present itself in the way we expect or hope it will.

I'm not saying I've found The Answer. Honestly, the truth I've discovered by turning inward and sitting with God in the silence and space of my own self doesn't look anything like I thought it would. It's a lot murkier, a lot less clear. Most of the time I feel a lot like a tulip bulb deep in the dirt. It's dark. It's quiet. It feels like nothing is happening. The truth is, this journey inward has often prompted more questions than answers, more unknowing than knowing.

But I think that's what Jesus intended when I heard him ask me to drop my nets and follow him. I think Jesus was asking me to leave my relentless search for concrete answers behind and release my clutch on the control I so desperately want and think I need. I think he was asking me to release my desire for clarity and direction because he knows what I need more than anything is to learn to trust. And the thing about trust is that it's not born in the moments of clarity, in the bright, warm sunshine of a spring afternoon. Trust is born in the dark, under the soil, in the dirt and grit, in the seasons when we can't possibly see what's next.

Jesus didn't give his disciples any direction when he called them (though I bet they would have preferred that). He didn't point out which way they were headed; he didn't offer any clear insights or answers or even hint about where they were going or what they were going to be doing. He said nothing other than, "Come, follow me," along with the cryptic, "and I will show you how to fish for people." Jesus' presence was answer enough. He asked his disciples to trust him with that single piece of evidence, and he asks us to do the same. Jesus asks that we trust; he asks that we trust that he is always working for us and with us and in us, even when we can't see any movement or progress at all.

### The Work of Being and Receiving

I've always tried to study my way closer to God. I've tried to form a relationship with him based almost solely on intellectual knowing—because that's the way I know: that's the way most comfortable and least risky for me. But that way has taken me only part of the way. Ann Voskamp asks in *The Greatest Gift*, "When do you find yourself striving, reaching, grasping, for the next rung to try to pull yourself closer to

God?"[3] My answer? Pretty much all the time. I have striven to be closer to God in the same way I have striven toward professional and personal goals, accomplishments, achievements, and success for all of my life. Striving has always been my modus operandi, and it's a hard habit to break.

But here's the thing: as John O'Donohue says, "You cannot dredge the depths of the soul with the meagre light of self-analysis."[4] As someone who has spent a fair bit of time in counseling and a whole lot of time with my nose deep in the pages of the latest self-help book, I resist this. And yet, I also know from experience that it's true. Counseling, self-reflection, and self-analysis are healthy, important practices, and they have all helped me tremendously, but they have taken me only so far. We cannot continue to seek in external sources what can come only from within: from God in us. There comes a point on the transformative journey when we must release even the nets of self-analysis and self-reflection and trust in the slow, unseen work of God in us. God does not need us to pull ourselves closer to him. Our relationship with God is not a matter of will or work. Our relationship with God is a matter of being and receiving.

God is already here, as close as he can possibly be. Like the power of life that's inside the dormant tulip bulb or the latent seed, God's Spirit—the power of life in him—is inside each and every human being on this earth. He knows each one of us better than we know our own selves. We don't have to study or strive or even know our way into relationship with him. We are already in him. He is already in us. As the fourteenth century mystic Julian of Norwich wrote, "We would be right to rejoice that God dwells within our own souls, and even more so that our souls dwell in God. Our soul was created to be God's dwelling place, and he who is uncreated is also the place where we dwell."[5]

The deepest desire of my heart—the reason I strive, the

reason I dive into every self-help book, the reason I pray, reflect, study, self-analyze—is to be in intimate relationship with God. The irony, of course, is that I need not work toward the fulfillment of this desire because it has already been fulfilled; it has been fulfilled since before the beginning of time. As a friend once said to me, "In the longing is the fulfillment." We already have the deepest desire of our heart. It's not something to work toward or strive for or try to control. It's something to simply be in and, as Julian of Norwich said, to rejoice in.

Nets can offer us safety and security, but safety and security are not always the better way. What looks like safety at the outset can end up ensnaring us. What looks like security can keep us from the true freedom into which God invites us. It is good and right to be attentive to God's movement in our lives, but it is also good and right to trust that he will make himself and his way known without our grasping or pushing, without our seeking or striving—without, in fact, a lot of effort on our part at all. This is not complacency or apathy, but rather, a receiving. We drop our nets in confident trust that God is putting everything right with us and for us.

Ten years after the boys and I nestled dozens of bulbs into the earth, Janice's memorial tulip garden still thrives in the back corner of our yard. Year after year, the bulbs cycle through the seasons. Every fall I pull up what's left of their wan, shriveled leaves and toss them into the compost pile. Every winter I look out from the kitchen window at the bare expanse of dirt, knowing the bulbs are there, lying dormant and unseen beneath the soil. Every spring I clear the dead oak and elm leaves from the bed to see that once again, the bulbs have pushed their tender pink tongues through the cracked and crumbling dirt. Every year I know the tulips will grow and blossom into a riot of color until they eventually die back and begin the cycle again.

The seeds sown by farmers and the tulip bulbs placed deep in the dirt by little boys' hands need time in the dark in order to germinate. We cannot see what is happening below the surface of the dirt as the snow falls and the winter wind blows, but we know that everything needed for blooming come spring is already contained in the seeds. The same is true for us. The fullness of life is already in us, even as we wane quiet. It's not up to us to push new life up and out. Rather, we bide our time in the winter of our soul, trusting that we have already received what we will need to flourish come spring.

# PART 3

# Spring
## *Awaken*

*I felt my life start up again,*
*like a cutting when it grows*
*the first pale tentative*
*root hair in a glass of water.*

JANE KENYON

CHAPTER NINE

# Spring Peepers and Maple Sap

*Only God could say what this new spirit gradually forming within you will be. Give our Lord the benefit of believing that his hand is leading you, and accept the anxiety of feeling yourself in suspense and incomplete.*

PIERRE TEILHARD DE CHARDIN

It's mid-March, and Brad, Noah, and I are walking the trails at Spring Creek Prairie, an Audubon nature preserve about twenty minutes from our house. I go there often, in all seasons, sometimes alone and sometimes with my family. There is something about the prairie that grounds me. Feet planted in waist-high bluestem, face turned into the relentless wind, I feel my smallness amid the vast expanse of land and sky. The prairie always resets my perspective, reminding me of the bigness of creation and my small place in it.

The Nebraska tallgrass prairie is not yet warming to spring—at least not at first glance. The land unspools in a drab palette of grays and browns—brittle sunflower stalks, crisp grasses, skeletal honey locust and cottonwood trees. Nose running, eyes watering, I trudge along the path that cuts a swath up the hill, the cold wind stinging my cheeks. A few steps ahead of me, Brad and Noah walk side by side, their bodies pitched forward, braced against the wind. My son's hands are thrust deep into his jeans pockets and the tips of his ears are scarlet in the cold. He hasn't worn a hat or a coat.

"March is really not a pretty time of year out here," I observe aloud. We've stopped to catch our breath at the top of the hill, and both Brad and Noah nod quietly in agreement as we gaze out at the barren land. Continuing our walk, we follow the path as it curves toward the marsh. On the boardwalk that spans the bog, the three of us crouch side by side, last year's crop of cattails swaying above our heads, salmon-tinted fluff exploding from velvet brown tops like insulation from an attic's rafters. On my knees, I peer into the still pool, desperate for a glimpse of a tadpole or a wriggling worm, some sign of spring however small, but the stagnant water is lifeless.

As we start back up the hill on the other side of the marsh, Noah suddenly stops walking. "Wait," he says, gesturing for Brad and me to pause behind him. "I thought I saw something move." We stand still, listening and looking. And then I hear it—the slightest rustle in the dry grass. A tiny frog startles from its hiding place. Another hops from the mud and then two more, and suddenly, all at once, a flurry of springing erupts on the trail, a chain reaction of small brown frogs pinging from one side of the path to the other.

The frogs, a Google search tells me later, are spring peepers, a type of "chorus frog" prevalent in the eastern United States and Canada. Barely larger than a nickel, this tiny frog lives primarily in and around wetlands, and its evening song—which some say sounds like jingling sleigh bells—is one of the earliest signs of spring's imminent arrival.

It's rare to spot a spring peeper, even in broad daylight. In addition to their small size, their mottled skin is highly camouflaged to their surroundings. You might hear the males serenading on an early spring evening, but unless you are lucky or very observant, you won't likely see them. If Noah hadn't stopped on the path when he saw the lightening quick flash of the tiny brown body popping out of the grass, I undoubtedly would have tromped past and missed the peepers—and this first sign of spring's awakening—altogether.

## Our Soul's Slow Awakening

The slowness and subtlety of my soul's awakening did not, I admit, align particularly well with my triple-type-A, Enneagram Three, "make it happen" personality. The productive, striving, achievement-oriented part of me had no patience for the early March pace of my soul's rousing. I wanted to get going, put a plan in place, take action, tick goals off my checklist. I had clear expectations for how this season of transformation would play out, and I was impatient to get started. But the soul awakens in much the same way that spring arrives on the Nebraska prairie—slowly, gently stretching from its long winter's sleep. We are apt to miss its earliest signs. We might walk right past its quiet beginnings. My soul insisted I move at its pace, and when I did—when I actually quieted and slowed myself to listen to its stirring—I felt it leading me into unfamiliar territory.

One weekend I decided to read through all my journal entries from the past year (a task equal parts cringe-worthy and illuminating). I did so with a highlighter in hand, looking for trail markers like splashes of bright yellow painted on tree bark. I circled a few passages and notes, but in the end, I didn't find what I was looking for in the pages of my journal. No clear arrows, no electronic billboards, no Siri prompts telling me where to turn next. What I saw instead as I read through days, weeks, and months of musings was the slow, quiet, barely perceptible work of God. Stepping out of the publishing arena had indeed created space for something else, but that something else was not another opportunity to do or create or produce, but rather an invitation to enter into what God was already doing in me.

"Doing things for God is the opposite of entering into what God does for you," Paul wrote (Galatians 3:11–12). Paul's words remind me of how much I prefer "doing things for" over "entering into." Doing things plucks my achiever strings. I like a plan to execute, boxes to check, and, most importantly, something to show in the end for my efforts. "Entering into," on the other hand, while not entirely passive per se, is an act of relinquishing. When we enter into, we surrender control, releasing our desires, our ambitions, and ourselves into what God is already doing, into what he has been doing all along.

When I read back through a year's worth of journal entries, I clearly saw that the whole past year had been a practice of entering into what God was already doing—and not only what he was doing in me, but also what he was doing in my place, in the people I know and love and in my community. I'd hoped to see an obvious path marked out for me, but I was surprised to find that while there was still no clear way forward, there had been abundant gifts in simply being, in yielding to and entering into what God already had underway.

## Arrive at the Ground at Your Feet

I had to laugh when, as I culled through a year's worth of journal entries, I saw I had written early on that I was eager to begin another creative project. I'd thought I was ready for the next thing. It's clear to me now that what I'd interpreted as readiness was actually restlessness. I was uncomfortable in the waiting. I was impatient with the slowness of my soul's thawing. When I did finally step back to observe, listen, and wait, I didn't much like what I discovered.

In the early spring of my soul, in the waiting and the quiet, I became aware of a low but persistent thrumming inside me, like a cicada's relentless buzzing in the background of an otherwise still summer evening. It was anxiety, I realized—not a paralyzing anxiety, but anxiety nonetheless. I was unnerved by the surprising realization that this anxiety had always been there, simmering just under the surface. I had simply never allowed myself to register its presence.

For most of us, the temptation when we come face-to-face with something unfamiliar, disconcerting, or downright uncomfortable about ourselves or our circumstances is to move on as quickly as possible. After all, who wants to sit with anxiety? Who wants to sit in the presence of grief or regret, disappointment or anger? This is precisely why we stuff our days full with work and social activities, errands, to-do lists, and Facebook. This is why many of us numb ourselves with alcohol or peanut M&Ms, with shopping or Netflix. We stay busy, distracted, and numb. We avoid quiet and stillness. We don't want to see—or feel—what's underneath.

Recognizing that anxiety is constantly eddying below my surface was uncomfortable for me to admit. Honestly, the moment that fact made itself known, I wanted nothing more than to grab a sponge and a bottle of Formula 409 and start scrubbing kitchen counters or the bathroom sink. I wanted to get busy, accomplish a task, produce a measurable outcome. Instead, I stayed where I was. I sat with the anxiety. I resisted self-judgement. I put aside my inclination to come up with strategies and solutions.

"Arrive at the ground at your feet and learn to be at home," writes the poet and essayist Wendell Berry.[1] It sounds lovely, doesn't it? But the truth is, being present to yourself is not always an easy or lovely practice. For many of us, the practice of being present to our own selves can lead to a surprising or disconcerting terrain of emotions—anxiety, grief, fear, anger, disappointment, bitterness, or regret, to name a few. And yet, arriving at the ground at our feet and planting ourselves there is, ironically, one of the most important steps we can take on the journey toward uncovering and understanding our true selves.

When I first moved to Nebraska from New England twenty years ago, almost everything about my new home was unfamiliar. The vastness of the wide-open landscape and dome-like sky felt strangely oppressive. The searing heat of summer and the bone-jarring cold of winter were uncomfortably extreme. The pace of everyday life felt too slow—even traffic moved more slowly, and I was shocked to discover that hardly anyone tailgated me in town or on the interstate. The people seemed too friendly and far too enraptured with the local university's football team. Even some of the food was unfamiliar. The first time I witnessed a new friend pour tomato juice into a glass half-full of Bud Lite I was aghast. *Tomato juice and beer? What in the world?*

Slowly, though, we carved out a life and a home for ourselves in Nebraska. We made good friends. We painted the dining room walls, hung our kids' drawings on the fridge, planted a garden. We learned to appreciate the seas of bluestem, the trilling meadowlarks, the big sky, the ever-present wind. We found meaningful, satisfying work. We wore red Nebraska Cornhusker T-shirts on game days (though we still haven't ever mixed tomato juice into our beer). In short, we planted ourselves in this place and we stayed. Over time, this environment—once so foreign and even, at times, uncomfortable—became familiar. We were patient, and slowly our hearts warmed to it. Over time, we learned to be at home in Nebraska.

Benedictine monks and nuns make a vow of hospitality upon entering the order. The Benedictines believe that all guests who present themselves at the monastery are to be welcomed as Christ. "Our encounter with strangers—the unknown, the unexpected, foreign elements that spark our fear—are precisely the place where we are most likely to encounter God," explains Christine Valters Paintner. In her book *The Artist's Rule*, Paintner suggests that we take St. Benedict's vow of hospitality and turn it inward toward ourselves. "Inner hospitality is to open our inner selves to everything we fear and reject in ourselves," she writes. "We extend a welcome to the stranger who dwells inside us."[2]

Though it had been there a long time, recognizing that I had anxiety inside of me was like opening the door to find an unwelcome and slightly menacing stranger on my doorstep. I wanted to close the door in that stranger's face and slide the deadbolt securely into place. At the same time, however, I know that acknowledging and even getting to know this unfamiliar, uncomfortable, slightly menacing part of myself is an important part of healing, transformation, and growth.

There is work to be done here, to be sure. But none of that work, no matter how important, can happen without first arriving at, acknowledging, and then staying in that uncomfortable place. We extend hospitality to ourselves—even to the parts of ourselves we don't much like. Just as learning to be at home in Nebraska was born out of the long, slow work of arriving and then staying in an unfamiliar, uncomfortable place, finding and learning to be at home in ourselves comes from the long, slow work of arriving and then staying in the sometimes-uncomfortable places in our own selves.

### Be Patient with the Process

I grew up in Massachusetts, where one of the first indications that spring was indeed arriving was the sight of galvanized metal buckets affixed to the trunks of sugar maple trees—a sign that the maple sugaring season had begun. I remember taking a day trip with my family to a maple sugar farm in New Hampshire when I was young—traipsing through the woods in the slushy snow, gathering around a tall sugar maple as the farmer lifted the lid of the metal bucket and let us peer down at the clear, cold liquid pooled at the bottom. He invited us to taste the sap, and when I touched the drop on my finger to my tongue, I was disappointed to discover the sap was not nearly as sweet as I had anticipated.

Later we made our way to the small wooden sugar shack, where we stood at a safe distance from the steaming vat of boiling sap as the farmer demonstrated how he fed logs into the fire and monitored the sap as it was being transformed into syrup. At the end of the tour my parents, my sister, and I squeezed into a booth in the tiny restaurant next door to devour huge stacks of buttermilk pancakes drenched in the maple syrup that had been made and bottled a few days before.

The maple sugaring season in New England is short and dependent on the weather. A balance of freezing nights and warm, sunny days are necessary for the sap to thaw and begin to flow down the inside of the trunk, out the spigot, and into the metal bucket, where it is collected and then boiled down to form the sweet syrup we pour over our Saturday morning pancakes and waffles. A particularly cold, harsh winter can delay the sugaring season, as can an especially cloudy or rainy early spring. Farmers pay close attention to the temperatures and to the maple trees to discern whether it's time to tap the trees. If a farmer taps too soon, the sap will still be frozen and won't flow. If he taps too late and the trees have already begun to form buds, the sap will have already "turned," and the syrup that's made from it won't taste quite right.

If you live in a northern clime, you know that nature awakens slowly to spring. It's easy to miss the first subtle early signs—tiny spring peepers camouflaged among the cattails, the slightest give in the softening ground beneath your winter boots, the thinning of tree sap just before it begins to flow. The same is true of our soul's awakening. After a long winter of retreat and rest, our soul warms slowly too. Like the plants and animals that sense the earth's quiet rousing before it is visible to most humans, our soul knows when it is time to begin to unfurl. We cannot hurry this process, but if we are patient, if we allow space for quiet and stillness, if we listen and are attentive, we will begin to sense these first subtle stirrings.

It's important during this slow awakening to try to be open to the soul's leading. If you're anything like me, you will likely have an agenda (and perhaps an open journal and a highlighter in your hand). You might have clearly defined hopes and expectations for what the end result of this season of growth and transformation will look like. My advice to you is to hold your agenda and your expectations loosely and try, instead, to "trust in the slow work of God," as Jesuit priest and philosopher Pierre Teilhard de Chardin suggested. "We should like to skip the intermediate stages. We are impatient of being on our way to something unknown, something new," de Chardin acknowledged. "And yet it is the law of all progress that it is made by passing through some stages of instability—and that it may take a long time."[3]

These are hard words. These are words we might not easily accept and embrace. The intermediate stages of anything can be awkward and uncomfortable, and the middle always seems to last forever (We all remember middle school, right?). The early spring of the soul's awakening is an intermediate stage, a "not yet" stage. We sense the stirring, but we do not yet know where it will lead or what kind of fruit it will produce. We stand poised on the threshold, waiting, listening and watching for signs, eager to begin.

Like the patient maple sugar farmer who waits for the subtle shift in seasons, we wait patiently through this early spring of our soul's awakening, watching for signs of thawing and flow. A farmer can't see what's happening inside the tree, and the sugar maple does not broadcast when it is ready to begin producing sap for syrup. Rather, the farmer relies on a combination of observation, instinct, experience, and trust to know when to tap the tree.

Like the maple tree, the soul will not trumpet its awakening. If we are impatient and tap it too soon, we will find the soul still frozen, unwilling to yield to even the gentlest pressure. We cannot force the thawing. At the same time, though, we remain alert and attentive, looking for the subtle signs of stirring, noticing where and how we are beginning to awaken. We watch and listen for the quiet invitation to enter in, and when our soul slowly begins to awaken, warm, and flow, we follow where it leads us.

# CHAPTER TEN

# Red Fox in the Woodpile

*Our bodies are prophets.*

BARBARA BROWN TAYLOR

My friend Michaella tells me that a mother fox and her kits have made a den for themselves in a backyard woodpile alongside the path where I walk several days a week. The spot is a few yards past my turnaround point, but, hopeful for a glimpse of their sleek bodies and bottlebrush tails, I stride the extra few yards each day, peering through the leafy fringe of hackberry and black walnut trees as I walk, wondering if I have the right location.

The first several times I stop to look, I see nothing; it seems hardly a leaf or twig has been disturbed. But then one afternoon as I'm riding my bike by, I turn my head in the direction of the woodpile—it's a habit now to glance over there every time I go past—and I spot her: a slender young fox sitting proud on her haunches in plain sight not far from the path. She sees me but is surprisingly nonchalant, seemingly unconcerned by my presence.

I stop and watch for several minutes, my bike leaning against my hip, as the kit explores her environment, pawing at the ground, lifting her head to sniff the air, nostrils quivering. She is curious about everything—the tree root half-buried in the dirt, the wisp of cottonwood fluff wafting by on the cool breeze. When I blow my nose, she visibly startles and then stares at me as if to question whether I was indeed the source of such an intriguing and obtrusive noise. After a few minutes, a woman walking by stops to watch with me, and then two kids on bikes join us, and for a few seconds we all stand together, quietly rapt at the edge of the path.

The next day there is no sign of the young fox, nor the day after or the day after that. Each day I walk the extra yards past my turnaround point and then stop to wait and watch for a minute or two. I scan the area, paying particular attention to the two holes at each end of the woodpile that tunnel beneath the haphazardly stacked logs and branches. Most days my quest to spot the young fox ends in disappointment. And yet, each day I stand a few yards from the woodpile and look, hoping for another precious glimpse.

Another whole week passes before I spot a fox again. This time it's the briefest flash of a bushy tail, the tip of which looks like it's been dipped into a can of white paint. I catch sight of it out of the corner of my eye, just as it's disappearing into the hole at the base of the woodpile, but I'm not sure if it's the same young fox I saw last time or a sibling or parent. I linger for a few minutes, but the fox does not reemerge from the den. The next day I walk past my turnaround point and again the day after that without any sightings. It would be easier not to go the extra distance, but I can't help myself from looking. This pursuit of the hidden and the mysterious feels important.

I wait quietly and (mostly) patiently at the edge of the trail because it's worth it to me to catch a glimpse of the wild mystery hidden under the woodpile. Despite the fact that there are no guarantees—I don't always see a fox; in fact, it's more likely I won't than I will—I am learning that it's worth it to make the effort, to pursue the hidden with intention. The shy fox, it turns out, is teaching me a lesson in how to seek what's hidden deep in my own self. As I wait for the young fox to show herself, I am also learning how to patiently wait to see what hidden parts of myself might peek out from the woodpile and emerge into the light.

## Showing Up at the Woodpile

I begin each morning by writing a simple question at the top of a fresh journal page, right below the date: *What are you feeling?* And then I wait, pen in hand, blank pages splayed open on my lap. In the early morning, waiting for answers to write onto those empty pages, I am stunned to discover I don't have a clue what I am feeling. *Tired*, I often write beneath the question. *I'm tired.* It's a start, and for two weeks it's my only answer. *Go deeper,* I prod myself. *There's more.* Fatigue, I realize, is often a physical rather than an emotional state. I know there is something more there, something underneath my physical exhaustion. *What are you feeling under the tired?* I write to myself. *What's making you tired?*

But the truth is, I don't know. I don't know how or what I feel. I cannot recognize and name my emotions. For so long—my whole life, perhaps—I've been so bent on doing, striving, accomplishing, and producing, I haven't let myself feel what I am feeling. In fact, I realize, I have focused so intently and so single-mindedly on doing, striving, accomplishing, and producing precisely *so* I won't have to feel what I am feeling.

*

In the wake of this unsettling revelation, I understood two things very clearly. One: it is not healthy or good to be estranged from my emotional center. And two: if I want to grow, to become more wholly my truest, best self—and, like-wise, to be my truest, best self with those I love—I am going to have to practice recognizing, naming, and especially feel-ing my emotions. I am going to have to let my own emotions teach me about myself. This, I understand, is going to take patience and intentionality.

My hidden feelings, it turned out, were a lot like the shy fox in the woodpile. My feelings didn't appear on schedule. They weren't predictable. I couldn't summon them on command. Occasionally my feelings were right there at the surface, easily visible and recognizable. But mostly they stayed hidden in the dark, underneath the scaffolding of my everyday life.

And so I returned again and again to the woodpile: the blank page and the question—*what are you feeling?* Even-tually, answers beyond "tired" began to surface. *Angry. Sad. Ashamed. Disappointed. Restless. Agitated. Joyful. Content. Exuberant. Hopeful. Dismayed. Despairing. Bitter. Afraid.* I practiced feeling the emotions, being in the emo-tions. Beyond trying to figure out why I felt a certain way, I resisted the temptation to overanalyze my emotions. Instead, I simply learned to feel what I was feeling.

Acknowledging and sitting in the space of our emotions is hard. We resist this work because it can be unsettling—it can give us what I call "the oogy feeling" in the pit of our stomach. We get this "oogy feeling" because we are being shown parts of ourselves that we are uncomfortable with, dislike, or fear.

If, for example, we recognize that we are feeling anger, there is a reason why we are angry, and we may very well feel uncomfortable or uneasy with that reason. If we recognize that we are feeling sorrow, there is a reason why we are sad, and that reason may be difficult or painful to acknowledge. The truth is, excavating and then holding the reasons for our anger and sorrow up to the light is likely going to reveal something about ourselves that is wounded and in need of healing and restoration—and that requires more work . . . work we may not want to do.

But this is important work. As empathic counselor Karla McLaren writes, "If you can empathically communicate with your emotions as the specific and brilliant messengers they are, you'll have all the energy and information you need to create a meaningful and conscious life."[1] On the other hand, McLaren observes,

> Without access to our emotional selves, we grow in this culture like trees in the wrong soil, becoming tall but not strong, and old but not mature. . . . Emotions are messages from our instinctive selves. They can be carriers of absolute (and often unwanted) truth. Although many emotions aren't welcome in most psyches, each of them has an indispensable function and something meaningful and precise to say. If we ignore and repress an emotion, we won't erase its message—we'll just shoot the messenger and interfere with an important natural process.[2]

In light of this, I now see it would have been very helpful for me to have been able to recognize and acknowledge the deep sadness I experienced when I was forcing myself to push onward in a career that was not a good fit for me. That sadness, had I allowed myself to feel it, would have communicated important information to me about myself—information that would have then helped me make choices more conducive to thriving, rather than merely, barely surviving.

As Katherine May notes in her memoir, *Wintering*, "If we don't allow ourselves the fundamental honesty of our own sadness, then we miss an important cue to adapt."[3] The process of allowing ourselves to feel our sadness naturally slows us down. You simply can't move fast and be productive when you are mired in sorrow and grief. This is a hard place to allow ourselves to be, but it can also be a fruitful place. In moments and seasons of grief, the extraneous falls away, and we are able to see more clearly what we need and who we are. "Sadness," McLaren observes, "helps you release yourself from behaviors or ideas that take you away from your authentic self."[4]

Brad recognized my sadness when he observed that my work as an author brought me far more sorrow than joy. But until he said those words aloud, I had not allowed myself to recognize, acknowledge, or even really feel that sadness myself. Instead, I repressed it. I distracted myself from my sadness with more busyness, more productivity, and more striving toward success and achievement. In fact, I didn't truly feel my deep disappointment, pain, and grief until the day it was forcefully released from me via the prick of the orthopedist's needle in my elbow.

Similarly, McLaren explains that because it can feel frightening, overwhelming, and deeply uncomfortable to feel and express our grief, we are inclined to hide it in what she calls our "airy intellects":

> Our logical and linguistic intelligences usually try to circle around and dissipate grief; they like to talk about death and loss, find reasons for it, and make everything seem logical and tidy, which is the opposite movement to that which grief requires. Grief asks us to become quiet and stop all forward movement so that we may dive into the depths, but the intellect doesn't know how to go deep—not like the emotions can. The intellect tries to lift us out of the water and dry us off before we've really immersed ourselves in grief.[5]

This understanding of the nature of grief and why and how it needs to be expressed helps to explain why, in the past, I've tried to write myself out of sadness and grief (and to clarify, I mean public writing on social media and in blog posts and books) and why this method of processing hard emotions has not worked particularly well. The bottom line is that we can't deal with sorrow and grief intellectually or rationally. We can't reason or explain our way out of it or steamroll our way through it. We can't simply craft a carefully and beautifully worded Instagram or Facebook post, hit publish, and consider our emotional work done. In fact, publicly writing about our emotions before we have fully felt and processed them in private is one of the worst things we can do, because applying our intellect to our emotions convinces us that we've done the work, when in reality, we've merely mimed doing the work; we have performed doing the work for public appearances. The real work has not even begun.

Our intellect so desperately wants to protect us and save us from experiencing painful emotions, it will do everything in its power to keep us from doing the very thing that will ultimately heal us and free us—which is to *experience* our painful emotions. And to do that, we have to allow ourselves to be still and quiet, to wait patiently for what's under the woodpile to reveal itself and to acknowledge it when it does finally rise to the surface of our consciousness.

*Practicing Embodiment*

My heel injury and subsequent moratorium on running was good for me, not only because it forced me to expand my interests into areas I might not have otherwise explored, like trying out the gym, but also because it prompted me to try yoga, an experiment that turned out to have an unexpected benefit beyond improving my flexibility and strengthening my body. When I first started practicing it, I assumed yoga would help me connect with my physical body, which it did. What I didn't expect was that much like writing the question *What are you feeling?* in my private journal at the start of each day and waiting for the answers to rise to the surface, yoga helped me learn how to identify and feel my feelings.

Prior to beginning a yoga practice, I'd honestly never thought much about the connection between my physical body and my emotional health. In fact, I'd never thought much about my physical body, period. Unless I was ill or injured, I'd rarely paid much attention to it. As a runner, I was literally able to run through any physical sensations and discomfort I was experiencing. I noticed my labored breathing and the occasional sore muscle or stiff joint, but by and large, when I ran I was disconnected from the physicality of it (in retrospect, this may be why I ended up with a chronic injury). The physical aspect of running was a blur of body parts working together, one barely distinguishable from the other—lungs, muscles, bones, tendons, ligaments, arms, legs, core, feet. For me, the whole point of running was simply to get through it: to burn the most number of calories in the least amount of time and then check it off my to-do list for the day.

Yoga, on the other hand, is intentionally slow, and it's in this slowness that I have learned how to notice, be present to and listen to my physical body. Yoga is much more about the process than it is about the end goal, so rather than focusing my efforts on finishing, like I did when I ran, when I am doing yoga, I am more tuned in to the moment as I hold my body still or as I transition from one pose to the next. Yoga is also about grounding—literally sensing the mat and the floor beneath your feet when you are standing in mountain pose, beneath your hands in downward dog, and beneath your torso and your limbs when you are lying prone in a resting pose. It's about learning to feel physical sensations in different parts of your body, as well as noticing the actual body parts themselves as you move or hold still. Yoga has introduced me to parts of my body—the undersides of my toes and the ligaments between my fingers, for instance — that I have never considered or even been aware of at any point in my life.

This connection to and presence in our physical body is called *embodiment*, and it's inextricably linked not only to our physical sensations but to our emotional well-being as well. As trauma therapist and author Aundi Kolber explains, our sense of embodiment helps us listen to our "felt sense," which, in turn, is a key to discovering and understanding our whole, true selves. "We experience this sense when we compile all the sensations our bodies are giving us to viscerally know something and create a larger picture of what's going on inside our whole selves," says Kolber.[6]

In other words, our physical and our emotional selves are connected. In fact, they are literally connected via what's known as the vagus nerve, which extends from our brain stem—the most basic, primitive part of our brain—down the length of our body to our heart, lungs, liver, and digestive tract. The vagus nerve affects everything from our parasympathetic nervous system—which includes respiration, heart rate, and digestion—to some of our motor skills, including swallowing and speech, and certain sensory functions in parts of the ear canal and throat.[7]

Not only does the vagus nerve send information to our major organs, it also *receives* information from them. According to trauma therapist Deb Dana, 80 percent of the information transmitted through the vagal pathways is coming *from* our body *to* our brain; the other 20 percent is information transmitted from our brain back to our body, telling it to take action.[8] This means that if we are aware of it and listen to it, our body will communicate a wealth of information to us, including information about how we are feeling physically and emotionally. The opposite, as Kolber observes, is true as well: "We must recognize that when we cut ourselves off from our bodies, we cut ourselves off from our emotions too."[9]

This is critically important because, as Dana explains, this 80 percent of information is embodied information—information that does not originate in our brain but in our body. "When we befriend our nervous system," says Dana, "we are also creating a pathway to listening to this 80 percent of information. Otherwise it's traveling these pathways anyway, but without our ability to tune in and listen and understand."[10] As I've become more attuned to the physical sensations in my body over the last several months, I have slowly begun to understand that if we listen to it, our body will send up both warning signals and invitations. When we learn to trust these messages, we are better able to discern when we are moving toward wholeness and integration and when we are veering in the wrong direction and perhaps need to course correct.

I'll give you an example. Back when I was still blogging, my friend Kimberly read a post on my website and messaged me with an idea. It was a good, strong piece on a timely topic that she thought would resonate with a broader audience. She suggested I might want to pitch the idea to the magazine *Christianity Today* for possible publication. I immediately set to work researching other online articles related to the topic of my blog post, reviewing *Christianity Today*'s submissions guidelines, and considering how I would reshape the post into an article that might appeal to the editors. In the middle of that process, however, I began to notice a subtle sinking feeling in the bottom of my stomach. When I noticed the physical sensation, I did something I don't normally do: I stopped. I paused a moment to tune in to what I was feeling in my body, and when I did, I was able to identify the churning hollow in the bottom of my stomach almost immediately. It was dread.

Although I feel dread often, it's not always easy for me to identify its source. Sometimes I have to tick through a list of possibilities, monitoring my stomach's reaction as I go along. *Is it something with Brad? With the kids? With my job? With a friend? Did I say or do something I regret? Did I make a decision I'm not comfortable with?* When my stomach lurches, I know I have identified the source of my dread. In this case, though, I didn't have to review a list of possible triggers. I knew right away that the idea of pitching this story idea for publication was causing my stomach to clench. When I realized the source of my dread, I stopped and asked myself outright: *Do I want to do this work?*

In the end, I realized I did not want to revise the blog post into an article to pitch to *Christianity Today*. I realized it was, in fact, the very last thing I wanted to do. But I hadn't understood that initially because I had simply fallen into my default response—*of course* I would pitch the article to *Christianity Today!*—instead of pausing to discern my soul's desire.

My physical body knew even before my rational brain did that writing and submitting an article for publication was not aligned with the needs and desires of my truest self in that moment. The pit of dread in my gut was communicating important information to me before my brain could process, intellectualize, and rationally understand that information. Because I noticed this physical reaction and was able to sit with it, tune in to it, and allow it to communicate to me, I was ultimately able to glean important information from it that helped me make the decision that was best for me in that season of my life.

Likewise, maybe you can recall a time in which you felt a sense of dread or vague discomfort or even that something was "off," though you couldn't quite identify exactly what. Maybe later you realized you had said something hurtful to a friend, or overlooked an important task at work, or needed to address a misunderstanding with your partner or child. That feeling of general unease, the "oogy feeling" in your stomach or the tightness in your jaw could be your body's way of communicating information that could help you make decisions that best align with your true self. Once you begin to recognize these physical sensations as your body's ways of communicating information, over time and with practice you'll learn how to translate these messages and, ultimately, make better-informed decisions.

Practicing yoga has helped familiarize me with my own physical body and the information my body is communicating to me. For example, when the instructor on my laptop screen instructs me to "notice my jaw" during downward dog, I now recognize that my jaw is a place in my body where I hold tension and anxiety, and I can take that information with me into other parts of my day. When I notice my jaw is clenching during a meeting at work or during a conversation with my husband, I can stop for a few seconds to ask myself what I am feeling emotionally. Am I anxious about something? Am I dreading something? Am I carrying unexamined sadness, anger, stress, or fear that is manifesting itself in my tight, aching jaw? The answers to these questions are not always readily apparent or available, but by identifying the physical symptom and beginning the conversation with myself, I have begun the process of identifying a feeling and the source of my unrest, which can ultimately better equip me to make an informed decision.

Practicing yoga has also helped me understand that while I am capable of high-capacity functioning for long periods of time, operating at a high capacity long-term is not in my best interest. I have spent most of my life overfunctioning, or, as Kolber says, "white-knuckling it"[11]—consciously or sometimes unconsciously ignoring internal warning signs from my body and mind in order to cope with situations that are overwhelming or not aligned with my deepest needs and desires.

This is how I ended up feeling disintegrated, fragmented, and on the verge of a physical, mental, and spiritual break-down at the end of my professional writing career. My body had been telling me—yelling at me—for months that I was physically, emotionally, and spiritually out of alignment, but my response was to white-knuckle my way through: to push harder and strive more until I simply could not push or strive anymore. Learning how to listen to my insides and allowing what I am experiencing to influence how I respond and act on the outside has changed the rhythms of my daily life in dramatic ways. As a result, I am happier, more rested, and more connected with myself, others, and my environment.

I spent the long months of my winter dormancy and most of my soul's early spring stirring showing up at the woodpile. This looked like paying attention to my body and learning from what it had to tell me. It looked like asking myself what I was feeling every day and then waiting for the answers to step out of the shadows. It looked like sitting with those answers and that information—and even more importantly, sitting with the harder emotions to which the answers and information pointed. And finally, it looked like beginning the long, slow, exhilarating, exhausting work of repair and restoration.

This was work that revealed things about myself I didn't like and emotions I didn't want to acknowledge or feel. It was work that prompted hard conversations with people I love. It was work that is in many ways just beginning and work I won't ever finish. It is work that will continue to push me, open me, and grow me in unexpected directions, ultimately bringing me into deeper communion and intimacy with myself, with the people I love, and with God.

# CHAPTER ELEVEN

# Prescribed Burns and Greening Bog

*Who would have thought my shrivel'd heart*
*Could have recovered greenness? It was going*
*Quite underground.*

GEORGE HERBERT

Noah and I are back on the prairie. It's April and much warmer today than when we were here in early March. Still, I am dressed in layers, because one never knows what the wind will be like on the open plains. When we start out along the mowed path, the skies are overcast, but ten minutes into our walk, I've already broken a sweat and shed my sweatshirt, tying it around my waist. The fact that we are walking through a large burned section of the prairie makes it feel hotter than it really is. All around us the earth is charred, the grass blackened to rough stubble, stiff and hard under the soles of our sneakers.

The naturalists who maintain the preserve had recently completed a prescribed burn. Prescribed burns are a regular part of maintaining a healthy prairie ecosystem. They are used to manage invasive species like smooth bromegrass, which, when it spreads, forms a thick mat on the ground, making it difficult for grassland birds to forage for food. Smooth brome also outcompetes other native grasses, eventually turning the prairie into a monoculture that is not conducive to sustaining a diversity of animals, insects, and birds. A prescribed burn can stimulate native plant growth by destroying smooth brome grass and other non-native competition that typically grows earlier and faster in the cooler temperatures of early spring, allowing space and opportunity for the native grasses like Indian grass and big and little bluestem that sprout in the warmer weather to grow at their own pace.[1]

I know prescribed burns are good for the prairie ecosystem, but walking through the post-apocalyptic landscape, it's difficult to believe that anything could possibly grow in the wake of such destruction. The air smells like an old campfire, and the toes of my sneakers are dusted with black ash. As we cross the wooden bridge spanning the marsh, we notice even the cattails have been burned down to two-inch stalks that jut from the stagnant water. At the top of the hill, we turn around to survey the landscape we have just traversed. From a distance the mowed path (which those who were managing the fire somehow kept unscathed from the flames) looks like the Nile River glimpsed from space, a swath of undulating green amid a desolate expanse.

The aftermath of this recent prescribed burn looks like a total wasteland, and yet, when we pause again to catch our breath, I look down and am surprised to see there are already subtle signs of regrowth in the soot beneath my feet. Tender wisps of green grass poke through the blackened, flattened vegetation. Now that the invasive smooth brome has been burned away, the native tallgrass species have room to sprout and grow.

And, despite what looked at first glance like rampant devastation, now that I am standing still for a few moments, I can see and hear that the prairie is, in fact, teeming with abundant life. An eastern meadowlark trills from a marshy hollow ringed with black willows misted in early spring's green. Noah and I sit on a bench and unwrap our peanut butter sandwiches at the base of a huge cottonwood tree, the newly unfurled leaves above our heads shushing like gentle waves rolling toward shore. A yellow warbler calls sing-song from the treetop, pausing its melody to tap at the bark for insects, its tiny body flashing copper as it flits from branch to branch.

Our lunch finished, we stuff the remains of our picnic into the backpack and continue our walk along the swatch of green grass between the two burned fields. As we stroll, occasionally breaking the silence to point at a turkey vulture soaring in circles overhead or the tiny blue-eyed grass flowers blooming like delicate stars in the char at our feet, I can't help but recognize that the prescribed burn is an apt metaphor for our own journey through the seasons of our soul.

In other words, sometimes the most fruitful thing we can do is burn it all down and begin again. Sometimes, in order to make room for the best parts of ourselves to grow and flourish, we have to clear out what's getting in the way, what's crowding out the slender wisps of new life trying to push through to the surface. That's essentially what I did when I quit my job as a writer. I burned it all down, and I hoped— desperately hoped—that something else, perhaps something that should have been there all along, would eventually grow in the desolate expanse of space that was left.

## The Post-Burn Landscape of Our Life

When we do finally summon the courage to let go of what we don't need—to burn down what's crowding our soul or inhibiting our growth—we might wonder, in the aftermath, if we've made a terrible mistake. The post-burn landscape of our life might look and feel a lot like the burned prairie in early spring: uncomfortably unfamiliar, barren, and seemingly lifeless. We've grown used to our tightly packed schedule and routines. Like the native prairie grasses, we've become accustomed to fighting for space in order to grow and thrive. But now, faced with all this emptiness, we begin to doubt, to feel afraid. *What newness and goodness could possibly grow here?* we wonder. *What hope is there in this vast wasteland?*

In the wake of my own prescribed burn, I intentionally resisted the overwhelming urge to fill the new space that yawned open in my life with something else—busyness, productivity, a new project, shopping, social media. Instead, in the quiet rawness of the new and unfamiliar space, I waited. I rested. I became quiet and still. I asked myself one simple question—*What are you feeling?*—and paused to make room for the answers to eventually begin to push their way to the surface, first as tentative wisps, later growing sturdier and stronger.

I was disappointed the day Noah and I went out to Spring Creek Prairie with the intention of enjoying the beautiful natural grasslands. I went looking for beauty and new life, not blackened earth and death. The truth is, a burned prairie is not pretty. There's nothing enchanting, uplifting, or inspiring about acres of char. It's depressing, ugly, and more than a little shocking to see such desolation and destruction—especially destruction that you know has been intentionally wrought. It feels wrong and seems to go against the grain of what's natural and right.

Likewise, standing in the middle of our own personally wrought wasteland, we might wonder, *Isn't there a better way? Did I really need to go to this extreme? Did I just ruin everything, every possibility and hope?* But the hard truth is, sometimes there isn't a better way. Sometimes burning it all to the ground really is the only route to finding our right way again. Sometimes we do need to take extreme measures to create the space for a better life to grow.

The prairie burned to black in early spring reminds us that even when we can't yet see the tender shoots pushing up through the charred earth, there is still hope in what looks and feels like loss, emptiness, and death. The burned prairie reminds us that sometimes, in order to make room for a new beginning, we need to burn it all down and begin again.

## Our Soul's Spring Greening

Yesterday, back out on the prairie, my husband, the boys, and I followed a chorus of spring peepers to the edge of a hidden bog tucked amid a stand of hackberry trees. The swamp water was surprisingly clear—so clear, in fact, that I could see patches of the silty bottom between the emerald-green algae hanging like filmy curtains from the surface. We stood with our feet slowly sinking into the soft ground, listening to nature trilling like a symphony of one thousand piccolos in the stillness. All around us, green upon green upon green shimmered in the afternoon light.

Eight hundred years ago, the German nun and mystic Hildegard of Bingen wrote about this early spring greening. She called it *veriditas*—a word she coined to describe "the greening power of life." In her *Illuminations*, Hildegard wrote about "the exquisite greening of trees and grasses" and the "earth's lush greening," concluding that all creation, and human beings in particular, are "showered with greening refreshment, the vitality to bear fruit. . . . The world is all verdant greening, all creativity."[2]

Creativity and fruitfulness—from the exuberant greening of the natural world every spring to our soul's own greening as it awakens and comes alive after a long season of dormancy—is evidence of the Holy Spirit at work and on the move, permeating every aspect of creation. "For Hildegard, the Holy Spirit is greening power in motion, making all things grow, expand, celebrate," says scholar Matthew Fox.[3] Hildegard also understood the soul to be the "freshness of the flesh, for the body grows and thrives through it just as the earth becomes fruitful through moisture."[4] The soul, according to Hildegard, is the source not only of our spiritual energy but of our physical aliveness as well.

Reading Hildegard, I am reminded of a strange plant Noah used to keep on the windowsill next to his bed. Often called the resurrection plant, *Selaginella lepidophylla* is a type of desert botanical that can survive prolonged periods of drought, losing up to 95 percent of its moisture content without suffering long-term damage.[5] As its water supply dwindles, the resurrection plant rolls into a tight ball that can survive for years, blowing around the desert floor like a tiny tumbleweed until it finally gets wedged somewhere secure where it can wait out the long days and nights until it rains again.

In its dormant state, Noah's resurrection plant looked absolutely nothing like a plant at all. Rather, it resembled a small ball of twine about the size of a head of garlic, its tan leaves tightly clasped into a dry fist. To the untrained eye, the plant looked unequivocally dead, and if I hadn't known better, I would have chucked it into the trash can. However, the magic of this little resurrection plant became apparent once Noah placed it in a shallow bowl of water. Almost immediately it began to unfurl, unclenching its layers little by little and greening up over a period of hours, until it had completely transformed from a crispy, desiccated ball into a living plant again. It still wasn't the most attractive plant I'd ever seen, but it was clearly alive and thriving.

After I quit my job and stepped off the treadmill of productivity, I entered into a long period of dormancy in which it looked and felt for a long time like nothing was happening.

Dried out, exhausted and leached of vitality, I rolled myself into a metaphorical ball and tucked myself into a small, protected space. All along, though, as is true for all periods of dormancy, there was much more going on beneath the surface than was evident. It turns out, all the small, life-giving practices I engaged in during those long months of withdrawal and retreat were watering my parched, tumbleweed soul:

The practice of Sabbath Sundays in bed with my books and my journal and my squares of dark chocolate.

The practice of painting my living room and the satisfaction I felt when I stepped back, roller in hand, and admired the transformation.

The practice of buying a plant, transplanting it into a beautiful ceramic pot and then tenderly caring for it over the long weeks and months of winter and early spring.

The practice of writing what and when I wanted and just for fun and then not publishing it anywhere.

The practice of asking myself, "What are you feeling?" day in and day out and learning how to identify and feel my actual emotions.

The practice of learning to tune in to my body and listen to what it was telling me about my environment and myself.

The day I stood at the edge of the swamp with my feet sinking into the boggy ground, creation greening all around me, I felt a greening beginning inside me too. Like the newly watered resurrection plan unfurling on my son's windowsill, I, too, was emerging from dormancy and unfurling leaf by leaf. I felt my fresh, resuscitated, newly green-again soul coming alive. I felt my whole body, mind, spirit, and soul singing along with the symphony of spring peepers, alive and whole and well again. I didn't know what kind of fruit, if any, this early greening would ultimately yield, and for once, I didn't need to know. It was enough to feel the slow but steady greening taking place.

## *Creation Shows Us How to Reemerge*

May is unseasonably cool and rainy this year, and I admit, I don't much like it. Ever-optimistic when it comes to spring, I've already had my winter coat and wool sweaters dry-cleaned. They are tucked into the basement cedar closet, safe from summer's hungry moths, and I grumble as I rifle through them in the dark, feeling the fabric sheathed in plastic as I search for a sweater to wear. I force my arms into the soft wool, resentful that I've had to raid my recently cleaned and properly stored winterwear. I am impatient for the hot summer sun, for warmth on my skin, for blue skies and bright days. Spring seems particularly slow to arrive this year.

And yet, I can't help but notice as I gaze out the sunroom windows that everything—the grass, the tender new leaves on the magnolia tree, the ground cover, even the weeds—is dressed in the most dazzling array of greens I have ever seen: celery, chartreuse, emerald, jade, pear, pickle, lime, basil, moss, pistachio, all punctuated by a single brilliant burst of color in the back corner—the Northern Lights azalea blooming in the exact shade of fuchsia I wore as a bridesmaid in a dear friend's wedding more than two decades ago.

I probably say this every year, but this spring seems greener, lusher, more alive than ever. This spectacular display of fresh, alive, growing verdancy is, I know, the direct result of the very weather conditions that are causing me so much personal angst. The unusual coolness and persistent moisture we are experiencing this spring in Nebraska, are, in fact, exactly what is allowing for the birth and flourishing of this breathtaking green. The earth is unfurling and ripening slowly, in its own time. The tender blades of grass and delicate leaves that would be at risk of scorching in the searing Nebraska sun are thriving in the gentle drizzle and the softer light of these gray days.

We need this kind of slow, gradual replenishment in our own souls. As we begin to warm to our quiet reawakening, we might be tempted to hurry the process of transformation along. Especially during this early greening, as we sense our newly replenished energy beginning to flow, we might feel the urge to jump back with both feet into our former levels of productivity or our former ways of being. Furthermore, our culture, which emphasizes productivity above all else, will insist we've rested long enough and that it's high time we got back to being useful.

But now more than ever it's important that we move slowly. We would do well to pay attention to our soul's quiet whisper, as well as to what we might learn from the natural world around us. Like the tender seedlings, too much, too soon, too fast is not good for us either. We will scorch or wilt if we bloom prematurely. And so we resist the urge to hurry along this slow reemergence, and instead, we continue to rest in the replenishing rhythms that have sustained us during the long months of darkness and dormancy. Like a tomato warming slowly on the vine, a hint of orange barely beginning to blush its green skin, we allow our soul its own slow ripening.

It's raining again as I write this, plush droplets pattering onto the patio umbrella, splashing off the hood of the grill and the metal chairs, dribbling from the river birch leaves, supple and shiny in their newness. The orioles and the cardinals have taken cover, the squirrels have dashed up the trunk of the pin oak to bury themselves in their nest perched on the highest limb. I wrap my cardigan tighter around me and watch the rain fall. The grass and leaves seem to grow greener before my eyes, and when I crack the back door, I smell the scent of Hildegard's *veriditas* releasing from the soil and the leaves and the grass as the raindrops land.

Last week, during a break in the rainy weather, Noah and

I returned to Spring Creek Prairie for an afternoon walk. When we got out of the car and stood in the gravel parking lot overlooking the hiking trail, we saw that the land had been transformed again. Not even a hint of the once-charred landscape remained; all was green, as far as our eyes could see. What had been burned to the ground only a short while ago had come alive. The slender wisps of grass barely sprouting through the blackened earth when we last stood here were now ankle-high, thick and lush and strong. Creation shows us how to reemerge. In the springtime of our soul, we awaken and begin to green.

CHAPTER TWELVE

# Thinning Zinnias

*A thousand half-loves must be surrendered*
*to take a whole heart home.*

RUMI

On Mother's Day, as Brad and the boys planted a crop of early spring vegetables—radishes, spinach, lettuce, kale, and Swiss chard—I knelt in the damp soil at the edge of the garden and one by one dropped feather-light zinnia seeds into shallow furrows, gently covering them with a layer of moist dirt as I went along. Zinnias, you should know, are the perfect flower. I love them for their sturdiness, for their relentless cheerfulness, and for the fact that they bloom abundantly in exuberant colors all season long, regardless of how much or how little care they receive from me. A bit of water during dry periods and lots of sun will almost always guarantee a bounty of raucous zinnias by late July, which will last all the way until the first frost in October.

While some gardeners like to experiment with new plants and flowers and vary the look of their gardens from year to year, I stick with the tried and true. I've planted zinnias by seed along the outside border of our vegetable garden for nineteen consecutive springs, not only because they are a cinch to grow, but also because they make good cutting flowers. All summer I snip fistfuls to plunk into bud vases on my desk, on bedside tables, and on windowsills around the house, and there are always plenty of blooms left in the garden to admire from my kitchen window while I wash the supper dishes.

A few weeks after I'd planted the zinnias, however, I could see, as I stood at the edge of the garden, that the spring's frequent rains, while good for the greening of the grass, shrubs, and trees in my backyard, had not been as kind to the zinnia seeds. Pooling water from several torrential downpours had apparently carried the seeds I buried on Mother's Day all to one side of the garden bed. Now, instead of sprouting evenly spaced in neat rows as I had planned, the tender seedlings that had pushed through the soil were all clumped closely together, one nearly on top of the other along the edge of the raised bed. They were too crowded; I knew if I didn't thin them out soon, few, if any, would survive to bloom later in the summer.

I sat hunched over the garden bed, knees in the damp dirt again, and slowly plucked zinnia seedlings one by one from the soil. The weaker ones with the pale, flopping stems were the first to go, but as I made my way through the clumps, I realized I would have to pull out even some of the more robust, healthy sprouts in order to give the growing plants ample space. I hesitated, my hand hovering over the dirt, not wanting to rid the bed of perfectly healthy plants. I knew, though, that it was important to thin them now, while they were still young and before they began to fight each other for water, sun, and nutrients. I plucked another dozen seedlings from the moist dirt, tossing them into the bucket at my side, where they wilted on top of a pile of weeds.

## Spring

### Forced to Make Space

As I write this, we are several months into the coronavirus pandemic—an event that has required a dramatic forced pruning and "thinning" of many of the activities that once filled our daily lives. Back in March, public health officials advised that we stay home in order to help prevent the virus from spreading at an accelerated rate. We were told to restrict our in-person social interactions and, when we absolutely couldn't avoid contact with others, to maintain a safe distance of six feet between us. Instructed to shelter in place, we ventured out only for necessities—groceries, gas, prescription refills.

Shopping, stopping at the library to browse the stacks, coffee with friends, dinners out with my husband, social events, church—all were plucked from our lives overnight. Restaurants, shops and hair and nail salons shuttered their doors. The parks and recreation department here in Lincoln wrapped neighborhood playgrounds in plastic orange construction fencing and tacked up "do not enter" warning signs. We hunkered down in self-quarantine, distancing ourselves from our colleagues, neighbors, friends, and even many of our own extended family members. I packed what files I thought I might need from my cubicle at work, loaded them along with a loaner laptop into the backseat of my car, and drove home to set up a temporary office in our sunroom. Little did I know, I would end up working remotely from that space for many months.

It was a deeply unnerving time; anxieties and fears ran rampant. I worried about my parents, who are in their late seventies and live 1,500 miles away. I worried about my sister's husband, who, as an ICU nurse practitioner, was caring for COVID-19 patients—many of whom were on ventilators, some of whom had died. Sometimes I lay awake for hours in the middle of the night, gripped with a paralyzing fear. During the daytime, worry was my subtle but constant companion. I carried it with me, a knot of dread in the pit of my stomach.

There was no transition period to ease us into this new rhythm of being. Our boys had come home from school for spring break and never went back. I erased every activity and event that had been penciled onto the calendar. My planner, once a blur of dozens of meetings, kids' sports, orchestra concerts, social gatherings, doctors' and dentist appointments, and volunteer commitments suddenly morphed overnight into a tabula rasa of empty pages.

I struggled with this "new normal" in the early days and weeks of the quarantine. Anxiety and restlessness simmered just below my surface as I grappled with how to live with so much more margin in my daily life. As the weeks passed, though, and I began to settle into a different rhythm, I discovered I rather liked my empty calendar and my much slower, quieter days. With my thrice-weekly commute no longer devouring six precious hours and with no opportunity to socialize on the horizon, I turned my time, energy, and resources toward engaging more deeply with new activities that brought me satisfaction and joy.

I practiced yoga nearly every morning. I took daily walks outdoors, not just to burn calories, but simply for the enjoyment of being outside. I journaled almost daily and picked up photography again, a creative outlet I had enjoyed in prior years but had let fall by the wayside in my busyness. I even challenged myself to write a poem a day for a month.

You should know, I do not write poetry. Prior to this endeavor, I had written approximately five poems in five decades. Poetry—writing it, reading it, or even thinking about it—has always intimidated me (even as an English major). I don't even really like poetry—despite the fact (or perhaps because of the fact) that my husband recites lines from Emily Dickinson on the regular around here. (The boys and I bought him a mug for Father's Day that says, "In my previous life I was Emily Dickinson." Never was there a more appropriate gift for Brad.) Hence, I was utterly shocked to discover that I loved the poem-a-day challenge. Let it be known, my poems were not good, but it didn't matter, because outcomes were entirely off the table. I knew no one would ever read my poems, which was exactly what made the exercise so freeing and invigorating.

Some days all I had in me was a seventeen-syllable haiku (one evening Rowan and I collaborated on a "Waiting Room Haiku" in the doctor's office). Other days I was able to take thirty or forty minutes to work on something a bit longer. Along the way, I discovered two wonderful benefits to this creative challenge.

The first was that writing poetry helped me be more attentive to my own everyday life. I found I listened more closely to conversations, looked more closely at my surroundings, and was much more tuned in to what I was reading and hearing. Because I was always on the lookout for possible content, my senses were sharpened and I was generally more perceptive of the ordinary details of my actual life. The second benefit was that, because poetry is by nature more concise than prose, I was challenged to think about my word choices more carefully, so my writing and creativity was stretched in a new way.

As someone who had spent the previous ten years of my creative life focused almost entirely on outcomes—book sales, Amazon ranks, social media followers, number of blog post shares—writing a poem a day for a month in secret just for the challenge and the fun of it was a surprisingly gratifying experience. I simply enjoyed the creative exercise, and when I turned the calendar page to the next month, I not only had thirty poems tucked into a folder on my laptop, I also felt a fresh creativity welling up from somewhere deep inside.

My kids—a high school sophomore and senior at the time—were home every day, all day, attending classes remotely on their school-issued Chromebooks. In the evenings as the sun glinted golden through the budding trees, the four of us walked Josie together. We waved at our neighbors and chatted at a safe distance, front-porch-to-sidewalk. Rowan and Brad tossed a tennis ball back and forth as we meandered. Noah pointed out the white blooms unfolding at the very top of the magnolia tree, and we drank in their sweet perfume carried on the cool breeze.

Many days I sat outdoors in a metal patio chair to soak up the warm, late-afternoon sun. Eyes closed, I tried to identify the birds by their calls—cackle, twitter, whistle, coo, tap, squeak, screech. Grackle, cardinal, robin, chickadee, blue jay, mourning dove, red-bellied woodpecker, red-tailed hawk. I opened my eyes to see how many trees I could identify by sight—river birch, honey locust, pin oak, crab apple, magnolia, Austrian pine, white pine, redbud. Lacy leaves glossy and soft, white silk blossoms, slender needles, pink clusters pinned like prom boutonnieres to a gnarled trunk. Walking by my neighbor's blooming pussy willow tree, hundreds of honeybees sounded like an ashram full of monks humming their communal *om*.

In many ways it was a relief to surrender some of my daily responsibilities to the forced quarantine. I wasn't sad to be rid of my hour-long commute or the overabundance of nonessential errands that seemed to swallow huge chunks of a typical day. I was surprised that I didn't miss browsing and shopping at Target and Kohl's. I was glad not to have to shuttle kids back and forth to multiple daily activities or attend a host of obligatory social events. On the other hand, some things were harder to let go: in-person coffee dates with friends; my monthly book club meetings (we transitioned to Zoom, but it wasn't quite the same); the occasional dinner date with Brad; the opportunity to travel beyond my own neighborhood.

The coronavirus pandemic forced me to dramatically thin out what had previously syphoned most of my energy and resources. In the early days and weeks of the quarantine, I felt myself resisting this forced thinning of my normal daily activities. And yet, as time slowly marched on, I began to see that having far fewer activities allowed me to grow those that remained in a much fuller, deeper, more gratifying way. I realized I had spread myself much too thin across far too many activities and obligations. My calendar had been full, and I'd engaged in a lot of gratifying experiences, but, I realized now, I had rarely enjoyed any to their fullest potential.

In the garden, once you pull out a plant and toss it into the weed pile, there's no going back. You can't change your mind a day later and replant what you have decided to pull out (unless, of course, you sow new seeds or plant new starter seedlings). Unlike the process of thinning out plants in the garden, however, we *can* add back in whatever we've plucked out of our daily lives. We get to choose which activities we miss when we are no longer engaged with them, and we can decide to add them back in if we so choose.

For example, I'm recalling the time several years ago when, feeling stressed by my crammed schedule, I decided to cut out most of my extracurricular activities in order to focus solely on my work. I declined social invitations, stepped down from several volunteer opportunities, and even informed the members of the book club I'd belonged to for more than a decade that I was taking an indefinite hiatus. In fact, I streamlined my social life so radically, there wasn't much of anything fun or entertaining left: it was all work, work, and more work.

No surprise, I ended up regretting some of my choices—particularly the decision to quit my book club. Turns out, I deeply missed our monthly get-togethers. I missed connecting with my book club friends, enjoying dinner (and wine and dessert) together and connecting over our shared loved of reading. And so, six months after I'd stepped away, I emailed the club members and asked if I could come back. I told them I'd made a mistake in cutting them out of my life. I said I hadn't realized how much I'd valued their friendship and our time together until it was gone. Thankfully they welcomed me back with open arms and no hard feelings, and now I know: book club is one of my most cherished, life-giving activities and not something I will be apt to pluck from my life again.

## Making Room for Growth

During "ordinary times," I had often compared myself to women who seemed to be able keep multiple balls in the air without dropping any and without seeming to burn out. *How does she produce a weekly podcast, write a weekly newsletter, write three books in three years, maintain a social media presence on multiple platforms, raise four kids, and teach herself how to embroider, while I can't seem to manage writing content for one weekly newsletter and a handful of Instagram posts?* I wondered. I felt like a failure in comparison, which only compelled me to push myself harder.

Being forced to quit most of my personal and professional activities during the pandemic quarantine helped me realize not only that I thrive best with less on my plate, but also that it's okay *to have less* on my plate: period. In other words, just because we have the *capacity* to produce at a high level doesn't mean we *should* be producing at a high level all the time. Doing less than others does not make us a failure; it simply means that sometimes we are a better version of ourselves when we know where our sweet spot is and then operate out of that place.

I now know that I thrive best with a lot of margin in my day, my week, and my month. This means I am more apt to be the best version of myself when I get up early so that I can have a slow start to my morning before beginning my workday. I am more apt to be the best version of myself when I take the entire day on Sunday every week to rest, recharge, and refuel before resuming work again on Monday. I am more apt to be the best version of myself when I keep my Friday evenings open so I can come home from work, put on my pajamas, and enjoy a restful evening on the couch. I am more apt to be the best version of myself when I have just a handful of carefully selected activities on my calendar that I can engage in more deeply.

In other words, I need a lot of space and a fair amount of rest, and when it comes to activities, less is more. The garden of my soul thrives when I have just a few robust blooms to nurture, tend, and grow.

The coronavirus pandemic has been catastrophic. Millions across the globe have fallen ill, hundreds of thousands have died, and many, many more have suffered financial, personal, and emotional hardships. This experience has profoundly impacted each one of us in ways that will continue to be revealed for many years to come. No one, I believe, will emerge completely unscathed.

And yet, at the same time I feel very lucky that the coronavirus pandemic taught me so much about myself. It showed me what I truly treasure. It helped me see who I am and how I want to spend my time, energy, and resources. In short, it compelled me to ask, in the words of Mary Oliver, how I will choose to live my "one wild and precious life."[1]

Our circumstances don't typically teach us the kind of dramatic, transformative lessons of the coronavirus. The radical forced thinning we experienced as a result of the pandemic is, thankfully, unusual. However, there will indeed be occasions in our lives when the practice of intentionally thinning our many metaphorical seedlings and perhaps even a few of our hardier, mature plants could greatly benefit us. With experience, we are able to recognize what, where, and when to thin in order to encourage other parts of our lives and ourselves to grow and thrive more wholly.

A few weeks after I'd mercilessly thinned my crowded zinnia seedlings, I peeked over the garden fence to check on the remaining plants. I saw that the seedlings I'd left alone to grow after I'd thinned out the rest were now flourishing—a knee-high symphony of healthy leaves and sturdy stems. The plants had filled in their allotted space. Some of the stalks, I noticed, had even snaked through the slats in the picket fence, reaching for more sunlight and open space beyond the confines of the garden. I saw that at the very top of each zinnia plant was a bud, its green sepals still clasped tight like a tiny artichoke, biding its time to bloom.

The crowded zinnia seedlings in my garden are a reminder that while pruning is a necessary spiritual practice, it's also important to practice spring weeding and thinning in our lives from time to time as well. It's not always easy to pluck out and toss something into the proverbial compost pile that's fulfilling or feels important or seems perfectly good, but it is often necessary. Like fall pruning, weeding and thinning make space in our souls for growth and for the blossoming that will eventually come.

# PART 4

# Summer
## *Bloom*

*And we pray, not
for new earth or heaven, but to be
quiet in heart, and in eye,
clear. What we need is here.*

WENDELL BERRY

# CHAPTER THIRTEEN

# Praying Mantis, Monarch Butterflies, and Mustard Seeds

*If you will stay close to nature, to its simplicity, to
the small things hardly noticeable, those things can
unexpectedly become great and immeasurable.*

RAINER MARIA RILKE

Bumblebees drone languidly from one sunflower's wide face
to another as katydids, grasshoppers, and cicadas hum, buzz,
and chirp from deep within the tallgrass. At the edge of the
marsh, frogs spring from the cattails with a hiccupping peep
and land with a plunk in the safety of the murky water. As the
sun sinks lower on the horizon, a barred owl's forlorn call—
*Who cooks for you? Who cooks for you?*—haunts the edge of
the woods as a chorus of birdsong unfurls like ribbons from a
stand of cottonwood trees. It's June, and summer on the prairie
is in full swing. From now through the end of September,
dawn to dusk, the land and air will sing creation's concerto.

Many people consider the Great Plains a kind of no-man's-
land—unremarkable, nondescript fly-over country that you
simply endure on your way to someplace better. I used to
believe that too. When I first moved from Massachusetts to
Nebraska, I assumed there was nothing to see in this land-
locked state but millions of acres of corn and soybeans, the
occasional combine grinding through the landscape, churning up billowing clouds of dust.

It's true that the prairie's aesthetic gifts, even in summer's high season, are much subtler than those of other natural environments. The prairie doesn't offer the awesome grandeur of Colorado's Rocky Mountains or the breathtaking majesty of California's towering redwoods. It doesn't enchant like Maui's lush rainforests or intrigue like the austere beauty of Utah's wind-carved rocks. The prairie won't typically stop you awestruck in your tracks.

However, in my twenty years of walking these grassland trails and driving these country gravel roads, I've discovered there is indeed abundant beauty here—if you look for it. I often say that the Nebraska prairie has taught me more about beauty than any other landscape I've experienced because it's taught me how to look for beauty when it's not obvious. It might demand a keener eye and ear than other environments, but there is indeed a bounty of treasures to be found on the Great Plains.

### Do You See What I See?

Noah stops suddenly as we are walking the grassland trail on a golden summer evening. He takes two steps back, parts the bluestem with his hands, and peers between the stalks. He's spotted a praying mantis poised motionless like a tiny statue on a branch. Training my eyes on the spot Noah points to, the insect finally comes into focus, its mottled, stick-like limbs perfectly blended into its surroundings. I am grateful for my son's keen eyesight, though I cannot fathom how he was able to glimpse such a miniscule, camouflaged creature at the brisk pace we were walking.

The praying mantis moves to the underside of a leaf and then turns, tilting its triangular, alien-like head and looking at us with seeming curiosity as we bend closer to it. We note the row of spikes lined up like the teeth of a table saw along its front legs. Though its spindly body looks delicate, a praying mantis's gracefulness belies its ferocity. They are voracious carnivores, known to hunt and consume other insects and even in some cases small frogs and hummingbirds. For now, though, unfazed by the two giant human heads bobbing nearby, this one seems content to sway on a leaf in the summer breeze.

Noah and I resume our walk along the path, slowing our pace to admire the wildflowers that paint the hills a kaleidoscope of shades: purple thistle; brilliant yellow goldenrod, sunflowers, and coreopsis; blushing milkweed; lilac echinacea; tiny blue aster. Stopping to peek over the bridge railing into the marsh, we spot a muskrat busily building its nest in plain sight. The creature doesn't seem bothered by our presence at all; in fact, it seems to relish our gaze, occasionally glancing up at us, as if to make sure we are taking note of its industriousness. We laugh, wondering if the muskrat secretly aspires to live in a glass-encased zoo exhibit.

As we continue our slow meander, I trail my hand over the tops of the tallgrass, feeling the wisps tickling like whiskers against my palm. The air is so perfectly temperate, our languid walking feels more like floating in a sea of warm water. We follow the trail as it dips down to where the mammoth cottonwood rises above the marsh. Sometimes, if the wind is just right, its rustling leaves sound just like bacon sizzling in a pan, but tonight the cottonwood is quiet in the stillness.

I'm heartened to see so many butterflies waltzing above the tips of the tallgrass, alighting on milkweed blossoms to unfurl their proboscises deep into the blooms. We stop to photograph a monarch resting on a sunflower, its orange-and-black wings like twin shards of stained glass. Monarchs have joined the legions of other insects on the threshold of extinction, but on this particular evening, surrounded by dozens of butterflies in the coolness of the hollow, we can pretend otherwise, at least for a few magical minutes.

High above our heads the butterflies spin and swoop among the cottonwood leaves, and when we stop to gaze up at the treetop, we suddenly realize the source of all the monarchs. Hundreds of them have settled in clumps on one branch. Until this moment under the cottonwood tree, I'd only ever seen images of monarchs roosting by the thousand in the oyamel fir forests in Mexico. I've since learned that migrating monarchs travel only by day on their long journey south to their overwintering sites, so they typically find a tree to roost in at night. This particular cottonwood tree out on the prairie seems to be such a resting stop—a chance for the monarchs, which travel solo, to find protection in numbers and lingering warmth amid the clusters of sunbaked leaves.

Noah and I stand beneath the tree with our heads tipped back, watching waterfalls of fluttering wings. We marvel aloud over the fact that if we hadn't happened to look up in that moment, we would have missed this silent, sacred spectacle altogether.

### Abundant Life Is Not One-Size-Fits-All

Back at home, our vegetable garden is exploding in a burst of abundant, exuberant growth. It's a jungle out there, in part because we've gotten complacent about weeding lately and have let the plants, both cultivated and wild, have their way. Mostly, though, the reason for the rampant botanical unruliness is simply that when it comes to gardening, summer is the season of abundance. We are finally reaping the fruits of spring's tilling and planting, thinning, watering, and weeding.

Standing under the burning midday sun, I breathe in the sharp smell of tomato leaves warming in the dry heat. I pluck Sweet 100 cherry tomatoes from the vine and pop them one after the other into my mouth, biting down to release a sudden burst of juice—hot and sweet. I crouch to peer through the netting at the butternut squash nestled amid its prickly vines, and I can almost taste the red lentil squash curry that will simmer in the Dutch oven on a winter afternoon, long after the garden has been put to bed.

Later, as Brad waters in the hot dusk, the pungent scent of basil and cilantro perfumes the humid air, wafting around the corner of the house to where I recline on my lounge chair on the back patio. We eat melt-in-your-mouth crisp kale chips with our burgers for dinner. A colander full of green beans sits on the top shelf in the refrigerator, and a zucchini the size of my forearm rests on the kitchen counter. We can't possibly eat all the abundance our garden is producing, so we share with our neighbors, ringing their doorbells with our arms full of squash, leaving baggies of cherry tomatoes on their front porches.

Our garden's summer harvest is a perfect picture of the word *abundance*. My online dictionary tells me *abundance* is defined as "an extremely plentiful or oversufficient quantity or supply."[1] Not just plentitude, but *extreme* plentitude. Not just sufficient, but *oversufficient*. Our contemporary culture insists that this kind of abundance in the extreme should be always be our goal: more money, more stuff, more productivity, more achievements, and more accolades are the name of the game. We learn early on that more is always better. We are taught to make excess our aspiration.

And yet, as I have learned to let go bit by bit of what I had always assumed was integral to a successful and satisfying life—my career and status as an author, my platform, my never-ending projects and to-do lists, my ambition, my

striving, and my endless busyness—I have come to understand that abundance and abundant life can look very different than I have been taught to expect.

God promises to give us life and to give it to us abundantly (John 10:10). I've borne witness to the fulfillment of
this promise in my own life, but I'm also learning in this
summer of my soul that "abundant life" is not one-size-fits-
all. Just as abundance looks very different on the summer
prairie than it does in the summer garden, abundant life
looks different for each of us as well. Turns out, abundant
life for me looks a lot less like my backyard garden right
now—with its exuberant growth, lots of variety, a huge harvest, extreme plentitude—and a lot more like the Nebraska
prairie, where, if one is not observant and aware, the bounty
of gifts can go unnoticed or overlooked.

When Brad and I were first learning to garden, I was
often envious of my friends' more prolific, well-organized,
and well-established gardens, with their tidy raised beds,
neatly staked flowers, and pea gravel paths. I despaired as I
paged through image after image of glorious personal and
professional gardens in *Better Homes & Gardens* magazine, looking up from the glossy photo spreads at my own
garden, with its scraggly rows of vegetables and unruly
tumble of leggy flowers, half their petals already nibbled
off by the rabbits. I wondered if my garden would ever look
even half as good or produce even half as much as everyone
else's seemed to.

Likewise, I've had many seasons in my professional life
when I've looked over the fence at someone else's garden—at
the size of their audience, their number of five-star Amazon
reviews, the Instagram photo of them smiling brightly as
they signed yet another three-book contract—and felt sick
with envy. I couldn't help but bemoan the fact that while
their garden was producing a prodigious quantity of fruit at

a seemingly astounding rate, I was struggling to produce a single proverbial tomato without a hornworm hole in it. In time, though, I have come to understand that another person's blooming does not diminish the possibility of my own. I also know now that there are many kinds of gardens and many types of blooms. Blooming does not look the same for everyone. The Gardens of Versailles are beautiful, to be sure, but so is a simple window box full of scarlet geraniums hung on the wrought-iron railing of an apartment balcony.

I've learned over the past year that living smaller, simpler, and quieter actually allows me to live more wholly and fully than I ever could have imagined. It sounds like a paradox, I know, but it is in this very paradox that I have found my truth. What might look less-than, unambitious, ordinary, and unexceptional as seen through the lens of our culture's standards and expectations has turned out to feel exactly like right-sized living and thriving to me.

The possibility of abundant living had been there all along, hidden within my ordinary, everyday life. But like the praying mantis camouflaged amid the prairie grass and the monarchs tucked into their evening cottonwood roost, I almost passed right by. In my hurried pursuit of bigger, better, and more, I nearly missed the hidden plentitude that was already mine.

Our understanding of abundance and what qualifies as an abundant life has been informed and shaped by the myth of the American dream. God's view of abundance, on the other hand, looks markedly different from what the world insists is the one and only narrative of success.

Take, for example, the parable of the mustard seed. I'd always assumed that when Jesus described the kingdom of God to be "like a mustard seed" that "grew and became a tree" large enough for birds to perch on its branches and build their nests in its boughs (see Luke 13:18–19 NIV) he meant that the kingdom of God starts small and unassuming but eventually grows into something big and impressive and noteworthy. In my mind's eye, I envisioned the tiniest, most humble of seeds growing into something spectacular and awe-inspiring. I imagined a majestic oak, its limbs and branches reaching high toward the sky and extending far over the ground, its lush canopy offering shelter for a multitude of birds and squirrels and other creatures. Except Jesus didn't say anything about a majestic oak tree. Jesus talked about a mustard seed that grows into a mustard plant.

In his book *Meditations on the Parables of Jesus*, author, teacher, and monk Thomas Keating notes that the mustard plant, while indeed fast-spreading, does not grow to the height of anything close to the size of a tree. In reality, a mature mustard plant tops out at about four feet high. Its branches might be strong enough to support a single, small bird's nest, but it's by no stretch of the imagination a tree, and certainly not the strong, tall, shade- and shelter-producing oak I'd always imagined when I read this parable. When it comes right down to it, the mustard plant is a rather plain, lowly, scrubby kind of shrub.

In this parable, Jesus turns our expectation of what the kingdom of God actually is on its head. The kingdom of God is a mustard plant—modest, inconspicuous, scraggly—barely one step beyond an ordinary weed. It's not outwardly impressive. It's not grandiose or awe-inspiring. We would hardly even notice it if we were to pass it by.

In other words, God's idea of abundance and abundant life looks very different from what our culture's definition of abundance and abundant life has taught us to expect. Our culture holds up the majestic oak tree—bigger, better, and more. God holds up the mustard plant—small, humble, ordinary. "The kingdom is in everyday life with its ups and downs and above all, in its insignificance," writes Keating.

"Such is where most people actually live their lives. The kingdom is thus readily available to everyone."[2]

## Choosing a Different Way

My youngest son, Rowan, has asked me more than once why I don't work full-time. "Don't you want to earn more money?" he asks. "Don't you want to *do* more?" He can't understand why I intentionally choose a smaller income and a part-time job when I could earn twice as much if I worked full-time. I've explained to Rowan that this professional and lifestyle choice is a privilege not everyone has. I am lucky. My husband has a full-time job that includes good benefits and health insurance coverage for our whole family. He earns enough that I can choose to work fewer hours.

"But *why*?" Rowan presses. "Why do you *want* to work fewer hours if you *could* work more and earn more money?" For Rowan, at least right now, more is better—more work means more money, which means the opportunity for more frequent and fancier vacations, and for the acquisition of more, better stuff. The fact that we've had the same thirty-two-inch, "not smart" television for the past several years is incomprehensible to him—why have something less-than when we can afford to have something bigger and better?

I've chosen the other way in the past—the long work weeks, the striving for better and more, the overscheduled days, the harried feeling that there are never enough hours in the day or the week or the month. In fact, I chose that way for most of my adult life. And then I learned that's not the only way available to me. I learned there is another way that is better-suited for me.

The way I choose these days looks less significant and less important by our culture's standards. I don't have a fancy job title. I clock in when I arrive at my part-time job and clock out before I leave, just like I did thirty-five years ago at the part-time job I had in high school in the kitchen of the local nursing home (except back then I inserted a card into a punch clock, and now I clock in and out digitally on my computer). I earn an hourly wage rather than an annual salary. My job does not offer "room for growth" or opportunities for advancement. There is no possibility of a promotion on the horizon. No one is particularly impressed when I tell them that my job is to write fundraising copy for a nonprofit organization.

Truthfully, there have been moments when I've thought, *Really? Here you are at fifty-one years old with no professional trajectory to speak of, still punching out at the end of your workday like you did in high school? This is what you have to show for yourself after two degrees and thirty years in the workforce?* Sometimes my professional life feels a lot like failure. But then I remember. My work is compelling and fulfilling. I enjoy the people I work with, which is no small thing. And fewer hours means a lot more margin in my days and my weeks.

I used to feel guilty on the two days of the work week that I didn't go into the office. I pressured myself to make the most of that time by being productive and accomplishing as much around the house and in my creative work as possible. Slowly, though, I have learned to let my foot off the gas pedal a bit. I allow myself a slower start on the days I don't work, with more time on the sofa with a cup of coffee in one hand and a book in the other, my legs curled around my dog. I tinker at writing this book, which will likely never earn me a dime, and I get great satisfaction in that slow creative work.

I've learned to choose gratitude over guilt. I'm grateful I have the freedom to choose the way of work that's best suited for me, and I don't take this privilege for granted. I tell my son that what looks boring, pedestrian, and less-than to him—the window box of geraniums versus the Gardens of Versailles—is actually the sweet spot for me. I tell him that the process of discovering his own professional sweet spot will be part of his ongoing work as an adult.

Turns out, abundant life has little to do with society's definitions of success or achievement. Abundance can't be measured by a sales royalty report or the square footage of our home. It does not depend on our job title, our salary, or how much we produce or own. It is not defined by the size of our television, the brand of our handbag, or where we vacation. In fact, abundant life for some of us looks a lot like the opposite of what we might think of as "abundance."

It looks small. It looks ordinary. It looks rather unimpressive. It's the hidden praying mantis in the bluestem and the roosting monarchs in the cottonwood tree. It's the tallgrass prairie in the middle of fly-over country. It's the shrubby mustard plant that looks like a weed. We already have life and we have it abundantly. But we might miss it entirely if we're not looking.

# CHAPTER FOURTEEN

# German Heirloom Tomatoes and Pumpkin Vines

*Soul growth begins when we actively embrace
ourselves, even in seeming failure.*

LUCI SHAW

In addition to an abundant crop of zucchini, cherry tomatoes, basil, and kale, our garden has also produced its share of disappointments this year, as gardens typically do. Earlier this spring, Brad had high hopes for a German heirloom tomato seedling our neighbor Karna had given him. The plant showed promise, growing fast during June and July and quickly spreading out over the length and width of the raised bed. Unable to contain it with metal cages and netting, Brad let the German tomato plant have its way, and he was thrilled when it began to sprout dozens of small, yellow blossoms: a sign that it would produce a bountiful crop of fruit. We began to dream of savory BLTs, tangy bruschetta slathered on crusty bread, slices of tomato and thick rounds of mozzarella drenched in olive oil and balsamic vinegar, sprinkled with fresh basil.

Turns out, prolific growth does not necessarily guarantee a plentiful harvest. For all its lush, sprawling vines and multitudes of delicate yellow flowers, Brad's heirloom German tomato plant has produced a paltry six tomatoes so far as we close in on the end of the growing season. Given its robust growth, he'd expected an equally abundant crop of fruit. But, as Brad wryly noted, while exuberant growth might lead to exuberant expectations, the outcomes don't always pan out.

## *Too Much of a Good Thing*

In hindsight, we realize that Brad's sprawling tomato plant undoubtedly would have benefitted from a generous pruning. Like the zinnia seedlings I was forced to thin after the early spring rain pushed all the seeds to the edge of the bed, there can indeed be too much of a good thing, even in a season of abundance. I've had to learn this lesson time and time again in my life, especially when I am in a season of personal growth.

When we are feeling alive and well and full of creativity, ambition, and energy, it's more tempting than ever to say yes to everything and to take on more and more and more— more projects, more social activities, more work, more fun. We sign up for new online courses, we embark on a new creative project, we agree to serve on another committee or community board. Full of anticipation and eager to experience the prodigious fruits of this abundant season, we embrace it all with gusto—until, that is, the day we stand back to survey all that we have planted and grown and wonder why the harvest isn't nearly what we'd expected and hoped.

Perhaps in our exuberance we've sown too many seeds at once or neglected to thin and prune, as was the case with my zinnia seedlings and Brad's German heirloom tomato. Or perhaps we've simply misjudged the season and planted at the wrong time.

The summer Brad and I moved from Massachusetts to our new house in Nebraska, we decided to plant a garden. Brad and I didn't know a thing about gardening back then, but we'd bought a house that had eleven raised beds in the backyard, so we decided, why not try to grow something? Brad planted dozens and dozens of pumpkin seeds that July—Sugar Pie, Jack-Be-Little, Rock Star—their names as enticing as the thought of the orange orbs themselves. Before too long they sprouted into dozens and dozens of pumpkin plants, prickly vines spiraling up fence posts, tendrils stretching to latch onto the garden gate. I began to envision pumpkins decorating my front step on Halloween, candlelight illuminating their carved faces. Pumpkins lined up on the fireplace hearth for Thanksgiving. Sweet pumpkin pie. Spicy pumpkin bread. Roasted pumpkin seeds, crisp and salty and hot on my tongue.

It probably goes without saying that all we harvested that year in our first attempt at gardening was a whole lot of vines. When our home's former owner arrived one fall afternoon to retrieve a few remaining items from the garage, we watched shock register on her face as she stood at the edge of the garden. "That's interesting," she said simply, clearly dismayed that her prized garden had morphed into a scene straight out of *Jack and the Beanstalk.*

Turns out, we hadn't known that July is far too late in the growing season to plant pumpkin seeds. We learned the hard way that when it comes to gardening, timing is important. No matter how great your desire for a certain outcome, planting in the wrong season simply won't yield fruit.

### *For Everything There Is a Season*

Many years ago, I worked as an assistant editor at an art magazine in New York City. It was my first real job out of graduate school, and I was eager to prove myself not only as a capable editor but as a skilled writer too. At one point

I had an idea for a feature article that I planned to pitch to the managing editor. I was excited about it, but after weeks of research and preparation, I couldn't work up the nerve to present the idea to my editor. I *thought* my idea was a good one, but I wasn't one hundred percent sure, and I was afraid I would embarrass myself if I was way off the mark. My lack of confidence got the best of me, and I never mentioned the story idea to my editor. All my research and preliminary drafts sat untouched in a folder on my desktop until I left that job for another opportunity.

Years later, with more than two decades of professional writing experience under my belt, I can see now that my idea had indeed been a good one and would have made a compelling article. I see now that I missed an opportunity to contribute a valuable piece of writing to the magazine. Back then, though, brand-new at my job, I didn't have enough experience to trust myself.

It would be easy, all these years later, to judge myself for lacking confidence during that season of my professional life, but the truth is, I simply wasn't ready to tackle pitching and writing a feature article at that point. It was still very early in my career, and I had not matured professionally. I was, in other words, still cultivating my soil—learning the skills necessary to work successfully as a magazine journalist and editor. I might have pulled it off in the end, but the experience would have surely been a painful one, fraught with insecurity, doubt, and anxiety. Though I didn't know it at the time, I can see now that it was better that I allowed myself time to mature and grow my skills (and my confidence) before leaping into the deep end. Turns out, I was still a little too green. I was trying to harvest before I had adequately prepared my soil.

If we are aware of it, we can see this pattern repeat in nearly every aspect of our lives, from our professional endeavors to our relationships to our personal and spiritual growth. Anxious for outcomes and results, and compelled by societal pressures, we often try to plant or harvest during the wrong season.

I recall another occasion in which I registered for a spiritual retreat with the plan to focus on connecting with and growing my relationship with God in a more intentional way. I packed my Bible, my favorite pen, and a brand-new journal, eager for the opportunity to hear what God might have to say to me. As it turned out, I spent most of the weekend napping, snacking, and paging through an issue of *People* magazine that I'd tossed into my bag at the last minute. Coming off a book release and several back-to-back speaking engagements, I was exhausted. My physical, mental, and spiritual wells were dry. It was not the time to enroll myself in a rigorous spiritual boot camp; it was instead the time to truly retreat: to rest, replenish, and allow the time and space for my wells to be properly refilled.

As King Solomon wisely reminds us, there is a time and a season for everything (see Ecclesiastes 3:1–15). There is a time to sow and a time to reap. Every season is not one of abundance, nor should it be. It's simply impossible to maintain endless productivity and growth; neither we nor the earth are designed for that. But the truth is, it's not always as easy in our lives as it is in our gardens to recognize the current season of our soul. We may think we have entered the summer of our soul, when in reality, we have barely begun spring's thaw and slow greening. Sometimes we begin to plant something new before we have properly harvested the fruits of our previous labors. Sometimes we try to harvest that which has not had adequate time to grow. And sometimes we push to plant when what we really need is to let the field of our soul lie fallow.

I have learned through hard-won experience that if we learn to tune in to the rhythms of our soul's seasons, we will be better able to discern what our own body, mind, and soul needs. Our needs and our seasonal timetable will likely be different from someone else's. We might be tempted to push ourselves to keep up with what we feel is expected of us. But we would do well, instead, to listen to the quiet whispers and heed the subtle nudges of our own body, mind, and soul.

## The Compost Pile

I'd like to tell you that the summer of the soul is always a season ripe with abundance, but the hard truth is, we can put in a lot of time, energy, and resources and do all the right things and still, when it's time to reap what we've sown, our crop—or lack thereof—might look markedly different than what we'd hoped for or expected. At the end of all our work and effort, we might end up with a metaphorical garden full of useless pumpkin vines or a sprawling tomato plant with lots of leaves and virtually no edible fruit. But here's another truth about our work and efforts both in the garden and in our lives: none of it goes to waste.

A couple years ago, Brad decided to start a compost pile in the back corner of our yard. You should know, I was against this idea. I worried it would stink—that I'd be relaxing on my lounge chair on the back patio, sipping Chardonnay on a summer evening while the pungent scent of rotting carrot peels and watermelon rind wafted past. I'd also seen a compost pile or two in my time and didn't much like the aesthetic. A steaming pile of decaying garbage and garden refuse in my backyard? I'll pass, thank you.

Brad, however, was adamant. Compost is the key to rich soil, which is the key to a healthy, robust garden, he insisted. He assured me he'd fence in the heap of rotting garbage so I wouldn't have to look at it and that it wouldn't stink because he would maintain it properly. How one "maintained" a heap of rotting garbage I did not know, but I reluctantly acquiesced to his plan, all the while inwardly harrumphing, convinced that he was wrong.

Brad was right. I don't even notice the compost pile. It's tucked behind a fence, and I've never smelled the stink of rotting carrot peels and watermelon rinds, even on the most sultry summer day. And the compost *is* good for the garden. This useless, unattractive heap of rotting plants, weeds, leaves, and kitchen scraps is actually the material that will help grow and sustain next year's harvest. The dead and decaying plants and other organic detritus we toss into the compost heap today will slowly decompose over weeks and months, transforming into the rich, loamy soil that will feed the seedlings we nestle into the ground next spring, which will in turn grow into the crops we will harvest next fall.

Nothing is wasted. Even our gardening failures—the fruitless pumpkin vines, the tomato plant that never produced, the withered basil that didn't get enough water, the spindly zinnia sprouts I plucked out—get tossed into the compost pile, eventually becoming the fuel that feeds next season's plants.

I've published four books, but I've also written proposals for at least as many book ideas that never came to fruition, either because they were rejected by multiple editors at multiple publishing houses or because I decided, for one reason or another, to abandon them. The rejection that stung the most was for the book proposal I wrote following the publication of my first memoir. I spent months writing sample chapters for a second memoir and laboring over every last sentence of the proposal my agent would eventually send to publishers. I was absolutely on fire about this book and couldn't wait to write it.

Unfortunately, the publishing industry was markedly less enamored with it. The proposal for what I'd hoped would be my second book was rejected by twelve publishing houses—and not only because my previous book sales were lackluster, but also because the marketing teams that considered it concluded my idea wouldn't adequately meet a need in the marketplace.

Needless to say, I was devastated. I moped around the house for weeks, depressed and weepy, declaring to anyone who would listen that my career as an author was over. Turns out, I was wrong. While I wasn't ever able to bring that particular book to fruition, I went on to write and publish three more books, dozens of articles and newspaper columns, and hundreds of blog posts over what was ultimately a ten-year career as an author. I truly believe every book proposal that resulted in an email rejection and every editor that responded to my pitch or submission with a polite "Thanks but this one's not for us" helped me grow as an author. These failed book proposals and pitches were the compost pile of my professional life. They became the foundation and the fuel for the seasons of growth and success that came later.

Through those failures I ultimately learned how to craft and fine-tune a winning proposal. I learned how to assess the marketplace to determine what kind of books would have a better chance of selling. I learned how to build an audience for my work. All those failed attempts at books and articles helped to make me a stronger writer and a savvier marketer. All along, even when I was "failing," I was honing my craft, building resilience as a writer, and cultivating a better understanding of the publishing landscape.

## Fail Better

Inked in elaborate script down the inside of Swiss professional tennis player Stanislas Wawrinka's left forearm is a Samuel Beckett quote: "Ever tried. Ever failed. No matter. Try again. Fail again. Fail better." After losing fourteen consecutive matches to Serbian superstar Novak Djokovic, Wawrinka finally defeated his rival in the 2014 Australian Open quarterfinals and went on to win his first Grand Slam title against Spanish player Rafael Nadal. It was Wawrinka's thirteenth attempt to defeat the number one–ranked Nadal.[1]

To fail better means to learn from your mistakes. It means that no effort is wasted, because there is always something positive—knowledge, understanding, insight, improvement, personal growth—that can be gleaned from the experience.

The fourteen times Wawrinka lost to Djokovic and the twelve times he lost to Nadal ultimately made his game stronger and fueled the way to his eventual wins. Likewise, the knowledge Brad gained from that first failed pumpkin-planting experiment was fodder for the next season, when he planted his seeds much earlier and, four months later, harvested a beautiful crop of perfect jack-o'-lantern pumpkins. The sprawling but mostly fruitless German heirloom tomato plant that will decompose into loam this coming winter will nourish the soil for next year's German heirloom seedling, which we now know will require a vigorous pruning in order to produce a bountiful crop of BLT-worthy tomatoes. The rejected book proposals still sitting in folders on my laptop ultimately helped me cultivate the knowledge and skill to craft three more proposals that eventually became three published books.

What's true on the tennis court, in the garden and in our professional lives is true for our souls and our inner transformation as well. The journey toward becoming more fully who we are is a messy one. There is ample discouragement, frustration, heartache, wounds, and failure to contend with along the way. In order to let go of what we don't need, we are required to excavate our shadow sides and examine the parts of ourselves we don't much like, and that can be a painful, difficult, uncomfortable process.

As author Katrina Kenison writes in her memoir *Magical Journey*, "There is nothing pleasurable about molting and shedding, nor should there be. In fact, I'm coming to suspect that the discomfort of release and transformation may be the price we pay for the subtle rewards of the midlife journey—hope, perspective, acceptance, renewed energy, and fresh inspiration."[2] The truth is, we resist transformation because, as Kenison notes, the process is often uncomfortable and, I would add, because sometimes it is even filled with grief.

We see this resistance to change even among creatures in the natural world who literally molt or metamorphose. We have a pet bearded dragon named Frill who lives in a glass tank on Noah's bedroom dresser, and every time he sheds his skin, which he does once or twice year, I stand at the tank equal parts mesmerized and horrified at how uncomfortable the process looks. The first thing Frill does, even before he begins to shed, is to retreat into his faux rock cave, where he spends a few days lying motionless in the dark. I wonder sometimes, when I bend with my hands on my knees to peer into the darkness of the cave, my face pressed to the glass, if he is in some sort of denial, attempting to stave off the inevitable by assuming a state of torpor. Or perhaps these few days of retreat are the equivalent of our winter of the soul, a period of dormancy as Frill prepares for his subsequent reemergence and transformation? Honestly, I have no idea what's going on inside his lizard brain.

What I do know is that when Frill emerges from the cave with his torso a patchwork of white, wax-like sheaths of skin in various stages of peeling, he gets to work. He spends several days rubbing parts of his body on the wood log and the rocks and even on the glass walls of his tank, shaking, shuddering, scratching, twitching, biting and then leaving a trail of delicately patterned, translucent pieces of dead skin, crisp and light, scattered on the sand. For a couple days, Frill looks rather unsightly, his body blotchy and scaly, his skin hanging off his torso and curling under his chin like a reptilian version of the Elizabethan collar. Finally, the process complete, a fresh layer of vibrantly colored, supple skin revealed, Frill then eats his dead skin, which is probably another great example of how nothing is ever wasted, even shed skin, but I'll leave that metaphor be.

We rarely recognize the process of transformation while we are in the midst of it. It's only in hindsight that we can see how far we have come and how much we have changed and grown. I read recently that a caterpillar initially resists the transformation process as it begins to undergo its metamorphosis inside the chrysalis. The caterpillar's immune system fights the formation of what biologists call the imaginal disks—the building blocks of the butterfly—because it doesn't recognize the emergence of these new cells and therefore interprets them as a threat. It's a little like how a person's body can sometimes try to reject a new organ after a transplant. The new cells persist, however, continuing to multiply and eventually linking together until they overwhelm the caterpillar's immune system, which ultimately relents.[3] We often resist our own transformation because what is being revealed in us is new and unfamiliar and potentially threatening.

There is no elegant monarch butterfly; no vibrant, new bearded-dragon skin; no beautiful, blooming, thriving garden without chaos, messiness, and even resistance along the way. In other words, there is no "becoming" without first un-becoming.

I see now that the messiest, most painful choice, the choice I most resisted and least wanted to make, was the very choice that made my transformative journey possible. If you had told me five years ago that the process of uncovering and beginning to live fully into my true self would necessitate quitting everything I had worked to achieve, I would have balked hard. And as you know from reading the earlier chapters in this book, I did not let go gracefully. I clutched at my status as a published writer. I held on and gritted my teeth until I couldn't possibly hold on any longer. I resisted letting go, and ultimately, I did so only when I finally understood that releasing what was suffocating me of life was the only way I could truly live as my whole, true self.

That said, I will also tell you that each season along the way has looked nothing like I expected. Every new season of my soul has brought unexpected revelations—some very good, many very difficult. And although I've walked through fall, winter, and spring, even now, in the middle of the summer of my soul, I still can't clearly see the way ahead. All I know is that everything I've released, every hairpin turn in the road, and every disappointment I've tossed into the compost pile has, in its own way and its own time, enriched the soil of my soul.

I know how devastating it feels when a long-hoped-for harvest comes up less-than or not at all. But I also know from experience that what we tend to call "failures" are also the foundation for our future fruit. We learn from experience what happens when we sow too many seeds at once. We learn from experience what happens when we neglect to thin and prune. We learn from experience that there is a time to plant as well as a time to rest. And eventually, over time and through much trial and error, we learn what we need to grow, thrive, and bloom.

# CHAPTER FIFTEEN

# Minnesota Cedar Tree

*I am rooted, but I flow.*

VIRGINIA WOOLF

Brad, the boys, and I are walking along a rocky outcropping known as Sugarloaf Point, taking care to watch our step as we navigate over and around the lichen-painted basalt slabs. I've been coming to this spot on the north shore of Lake Superior in Minnesota since I first met Brad, back when we were in graduate school. His family owns a cabin a few miles up the road from this scenic nature preserve, and every summer, we drive the eleven hours from the blistering heat of Nebraska to this northern clime, where the air smells like Douglas fir and the breeze carries the damp chill of ice-cold lake water. Each summer when we arrive for our week-long vacation, I'm always surprised to see the lilacs are in bloom. They've long come and gone in Nebraska, but spring and summer arrive much later in northern Minnesota.

Today we've emerged from the birch-and-aspen woods, picked our way across a cobblestone beach strewn with sun-bleached, water-smoothed driftwood and followed the trail out to the point. Hiking here requires that we keep our eyes focused on the ground at all times. The uneven terrain is eroded in spots, the soil and crumbling rock dropping steeply off the edge of the cliffs to Lake Superior's frigid, angry waves below. Though it's July, the wind off the lake feels arctic, and I find myself wishing I'd worn another layer. As always, I've underestimated the cold, forgetting that summer in Minnesota is not like summer elsewhere.

Halfway out to the end of the point we stop to inspect a cedar tree that's blown over in a storm. We marvel over the fact that, despite the apparent trauma, it still seems to be flourishing. The trunk has splintered at the base, so instead of growing up straight and tall, it now juts horizontally out over the edge of the cliff. But then, rather than staying suspended in a straight line over the water, the trunk makes a sharp right angle and begins to grow vertically toward the sky again. Branches with lush sprays of fan-like greenery sprout all the way up the length of its trunk to its crown. Against all odds and in spite of its tenuous grasp on the edge of the cliff, the tree is thriving.

Brad and the boys continue on, but I linger for a few more minutes, snapping pictures of the weathered cedar tree. I am intrigued by its resilience. The roots, I notice, are visible at my feet, winding like dozens of undulating tributaries in and out of the soft understory. At the edge of the cliff, where the soil has eroded away, they clutch at the earth like arthritic fingers, bony and gnarled. I nudge the toe of my hiking boot against one of the larger roots and am surprised to find it is rock-solid. Knocked over by a ferocious storm, the roots hold strong, still anchored in spite of everything.

### The Process Is the Point

Over the past few months I've been trying a new-to-me contemplative practice called centering prayer. The mechanics of the practice are simple, at least in theory. You sit silently with your eyes closed in a quiet spot for twenty minutes, during which, when your mind inevitably wanders, you gently bring it back to the present moment, often by repeating a word you have chosen as an anchor.

Thomas Keating defines centering prayer as the act of relating to God beyond thoughts, feelings, and particular acts. "The only initiative we take during the period of centering prayer is to maintain our intention of consenting to the presence and action of God within," he writes in *Open Heart, Open Mind*.[1] When I first read this, I paused at Keating's word *consenting* to consider its implications. To consent to someone is to give permission to that person, to yield to or allow that person to be the one in charge. In other words, we take action when we engage in centering prayer, but that action is passive: we relinquish control and allow God to be God, receiving him in whatever way he presents himself—or does not present himself—to us.

It sounds blessedly simple, doesn't it? And yet, as someone who has been a doer and a producer and a "make things happen" kind of person my entire life, the practice of centering prayer is one of the hardest things I've ever done. Yielding to the presence of God in centering prayer is a 180-degree turn from the way I've lived life—including the way I've lived my spiritual life, which has always had its foundation in my own efforts and actions. For most of my adult life I have attempted to study my way into relationship with God through a variety of avenues: reading the Bible, participating in Bible study groups, reading Christian self-help and other spiritual books, attending church services. But the practice of centering prayer is different in that it has very little to do with me. Centering prayer is all God; my role is to be present to and receive him if and when he chooses to reveal himself to me.

I settle into the wicker chair in the corner of my bedroom, eyes closed, palms resting open in my lap. Outside the closed window, I hear the muffled voices of two men chatting on the golf course, the sharp clack of a metal club striking the ball. A blue jay shrieks. One floor below me, a kitchen cabinet closes, and I suddenly remember that I haven't eaten lunch, which explains why I also hear and feel my stomach rumbling. I become aware that I am thinking, my thoughts lighting up like the flashing bulbs in a pinball machine, and so I repeat the anchor word I have chosen for these moments to return me to a posture of reception. *Open.* Breathe in. *Open.* Breathe out. *Open.* I concentrate on the fireworks of colors and patterns behind my eyelids. I see the imprint of my bedroom window, a bright rectangle drifting like a slow-moving kite across the black space.

"Receiving is one of the most difficult kinds of activity there is," Keating acknowledges. As he's quick to point out, "Receptivity is not inactivity. It is real activity but not effort in the ordinary sense of the world. It is not trying; it is waiting."[2]

Mostly what I've experienced so far in my forays into centering prayer is that, given a few minutes of silence and stillness, my brain immediately begins to act like the baby squirrel who lives in my backyard—all tumbly and twirly, running in circles, leaping, dancing, falling down, chasing its own tail, twitching and itching and then startling with a visceral shiver, like it's just caught sight of a cougar out of the corner of its eye. There have been many, many times when I have ended a session of centering prayer feeling frustrated and discouraged, convinced that the practice is a complete waste of time.

But I keep coming back to the fact that centering prayer is exactly that: a practice—a process—not a one-and-done accomplishment with a beginning, a middle, and an end result. I try to remind myself that there really is no goal, no expected outcome. The process itself is the whole point.

*Posturing Ourselves to Await Healing*

In the Gospel of John, we hear about a man who has lain ill and incapacitated next to a spring of healing water for thirty-eight years, waiting for someone to help him into the pool (see John 5:1–15). When Jesus approaches the man lying prone on his mat near the water, he asks the man if he desires to get well—to be cured of his longtime infirmity—and then he instructs the man to stand up, pick up his mat, and walk. The man obeys. He stands, rolls up the mat upon which he has lain for more than three decades, and, instantly healed, walks to the temple to tell the story of his miracle to anyone who will listen.

Similarly, in the Gospel of Luke we hear about a blind beggar who sits on the side of the road as Jesus passes by on his way to Jericho (Luke 18:35–43; see also Mark 10:46–52 and Matthew 20:29–34). "Jesus, Son of David, have mercy on me!" the man cries out, desperate to attract Jesus' attention. Despite the attempts of the crowd to quiet him, the blind man continues to call out to Jesus. When Jesus hears his cries, he demands that the blind man be brought to him, and he immediately heals him of his blindness.

"We ultimately don't heal, transform or create ourselves," writes Sue Monk Kidd. Rather, "we posture ourselves in ways that allow God to heal, transform and create us."[3] The ill man positioned himself on his mat near the pool of Bethesda and waited thirty-eight years for the presence of God. We don't know how long the blind beggar sat by the side of the road, but we do know he was there, waiting, when Jesus passed by. In both cases, the men were ready for Jesus when he arrived—poised and open to receive Jesus' healing.

Centering prayer has become one of the ways I attempt to place myself in a posture of openness and receptivity to God. In those twenty minutes of silence and stillness,

I am the man waiting by the pool of Bethesda; I am the beggar waiting by the side of the road. As someone who has spent decades trying, through my own efforts, to make my spiritual life richer and deeper—in essence, trying to make a relationship with God happen—assuming a posture of receptivity, of waiting, feels unnatural, unfamiliar, and even, on some days, futile. *What am I even waiting for?* I wonder. *What does "receiving God" feel like? Will I know when it happens?*

As I ponder these questions I wonder if they are perhaps too logical, too black and white. Maybe the experience of God can't be defined, shaped, or contained by my rational consciousness. Maybe this right here, this amorphous, feels-like-nothing experience *is* the experience. Honestly, I have absolutely no idea. The truth is, I don't see much progress in my centering prayer practice, at least progress that can be measured in any tangible way, but I persist nonetheless, opening myself to the possibility that something *is* happening, something I can't yet recognize or understand, something deep at the core of me that is helping to anchor me in my true self and in God.

Thomas Keating called centering prayer a kind of anointing, "the fruits of which will appear later in ways that are indirect: in your gentleness, peace and willingness to surrender to God in everything that happens."[4] In other words, God often works in us without our observing it or recognizing it in the moment. And so I am trusting in this unseen and unfelt anointing, trusting that God is working in me in ways I cannot discern, perhaps even in ways that won't ever be completely revealed to me. I am practicing a posture of receptivity, and in doing so, I am learning how to let God be God.

## As Yourself

In his book *The Wisdom Pattern*, Franciscan priest Richard Rohr suggests that "we would all do well to get in touch with our own operative worldview"[5]—the lens through which we look at the world and through which we understand ourselves. This lens, Rohr explains, is "a matrix of culturally inherited qualities, family influences, and other life experiences."[6]

It's not easy for most of us to objectively identify and name our operative worldview—what Rohr calls "the grid of [our] deepest experience"[7]—but it's imperative if we truly desire to become who we are. My operative worldview for most of my life has been the belief that I had to earn my place in the world. I believed I had to prove my value and worthiness, and the onus was on me to make it happen. I believed I could earn my worth by being a successful person—successful as a writer, a mother, a wife, a daughter, a friend, a Christian, and as a member of society.

Recently I was talking with my spiritual director, Patty, over Zoom. I don't recall the specific topic of our conversation, but I do remember quoting what Jesus called the second greatest commandment: "Love your neighbor as yourself." Except here's the thing: when I quoted the verse to Patty, I abbreviated it to "Love your neighbor," and left it at that.

As I continued talking, Patty gently interrupted me. "You know there's more to that verse, right?" she asked. "You didn't quote the whole thing. What's the rest of it?"

I paused. "Right," I answered. "It's 'love your neighbor *as yourself.*'" I paused again, realizing something that seemed important. "I always leave off the second part of that verse," I said, meeting Patty's eye on the other side of my screen. "I always leave off the 'as yourself.'"

I realized that day that I don't include the second part of that verse because it doesn't align with my operative worldview. If I live out of the belief that I have to earn my worthiness, then it stands to reason that one of the best ways I can do that is to love my neighbor. Loving others makes me worthy of God's love. Hard stop. I've never factored loving myself into the equation.

I have only recently come to understand that our capacity to truly love our neighbor grows out of our ability to love ourselves, which, in turn, grows out of our core foundational understanding that God loves us. God loves us no matter what, no strings attached. God's love for us is the roots of our tree, anchoring us, holding us steady even as the winds beat at our shores, even as the soil in which we are planted erodes. God's love is the foundation that holds everything together.

We can't get the "love others" part right until we get the "love yourself" part right first. And we can't love our own self unless we let God shift our operative worldview. As Rohr writes, "Unless we can allow the gospel to move into that deepest level of the unconscious and touch our operative worldviews, nothing substantial is going to change. It will only be rearranging the furniture, not constructing a new room. Conversion is about constructing a new room, or maybe even a whole new house."[8]

Practicing centering prayer is one way I am learning how to allow the gospel—God—to move into the deepest level of my unconscious. It is a practice that is helping me learn how to anchor myself in God and in his unwavering love.

Sometimes—certainly not always, but sometimes—when I practice centering prayer, I feel myself begin to slip under the surface layer of my consciousness, under my baby squirrel brain. For a few seconds I find myself in a deeper place—a place where roles, titles, masks, and identities fade away; a place where all the doing recedes. In this place of deep stillness, I feel simultaneously like I am nothing and everything. I feel like I am being cradled within a protected womb while at the same time opening into the infinite expanse of the universe.

By anchoring into the deep center of God's love for even a few seconds, I am, bit by bit, letting go of the flawed operative worldview I have lived by for most of my life. I am learning to consent to God, to receive him while also knowing in the deepest part of me that he is always already there. I am learning that I do not have to entice God to hold me because he has been holding me all along.

### Anchored

After a long season of letting go, followed by a season of retreating into hibernation and rest and finally a season in which I began to reemerge, sustained and refreshed, I expected the summer of my soul to culminate in something big and dramatic. *Will I uncover a brand-new, second-half-of-life vocation?* I wondered. Perhaps a new passion, gift, or path would be revealed? I could hardly wait to see what amazing and significant fruit would be born out of this transformative process. What my summer of the soul is teaching me, however, is that I am still in many ways operating out of an outcome- and results-oriented mindset.

"As you live in union with me as your source, fruitfulness will stream from within you," Jesus told his disciples (John 15:5 TPT). It turns out, Jesus' understanding of "fruit" and "fruitfulness" differs markedly from mine. I've always believed that a person was "fruitful" only if he or she was producing something tangible. In this summer of my soul, however, I am discovering a much different definition of fruitfulness—a counter-cultural kind of fruit that is less the product of doing, striving, and producing, and more the result of simply abiding.

Turns out, there is no dramatic be-all and end-all out-come in this summer of my soul. The fruit streaming from within is largely invisible to anyone but me. No new sec-ond-half-of-life vocation has been uncovered. No new pas-sion, gift, or path has been revealed. In fact, looking at my life from the outside, you wouldn't know that anything had changed at all. I still work the same part-time job. I still walk the same four-mile route several times a week for exercise. I still eat sixteen almonds every day at 10:00 a.m. I still live in the middle of fly-over country. I'm still writing—albeit without a book contract or a deadline this time.

And yet, at the same time, I *feel* different on the inside. There is both a lightness and a solidity in my body and spirit. I feel both rooted and free, small and expansive, vulnerable and strong. In this summer of my soul, a season that looks nothing like I thought it would, I am the wind-whipped and storm-blown cedar tree at Sugarloaf Point. I am still growing, though it is in a new, unexpected direction. I am anchored by roots that hold strong, secure in a deep know-ing that I am loved not for what I do, but for who I am, for who I have always been, for who I am still becoming.

# Becoming Who We Already Are

*We shall not cease from exploration, and the end*
*of all our exploring will be to arrive where we*
*started and to know the place for the first time.*

T.S. ELIOT

When my kids were young they received a monarch chrysalis hatching kit as a gift from their grandparents. The kit contained everything necessary to raise a "family" of monarch butterflies right in our own home, including a netted habitat and a certificate to order caterpillars to be delivered to our doorstep by mail. When the caterpillars arrived, we placed them in the habitat, supplied them with twigs and branches to perch on and enough milkweed leaves and blooms for a weeks-long feast, and then sat back to watch what would happen.

We set their netted dome on a side table in our living room and observed as the once tiny, translucent larvae munched their way through leaf after leaf and grew into plump, yellow-and-black-striped, many-legged caterpillars. We watched as each caterpillar eventually spun a silky hook from which to suspend itself from the roof of the nylon dome. We watched, rapt, as one by one each caterpillar folded itself in half and then split its skin apart to reveal a hard, jade-green chrysalis underneath.

After a few days of staring at the stagnant chrysalises, we

lost interest. A chrysalis doesn't do anything except hang motionless from whatever it's affixed to for ten or so days, so there wasn't much to see. We checked in once or twice a day to see if anything was stirring, but for the most part, we ignored the chrysalises in our living room.

Unbeknownst to us, however, there was a lot happening inside those hard casings hanging motionless inside the tent. Though we couldn't see it, the caterpillars were undergoing a complex transformation as they literally dissolved into liquid inside their chrysalises and then began rapidly dividing their cells, using the protein-rich "soup" to create their new body parts, from wings and legs to eyes and antennae.

Ten days after retreating into their chrysalises, our monarch butterflies began to show signs of hatching. The once-green shells darkened and then turned translucent. Inside, we could see the orange and black wings of the butterflies. Soon after, the monarchs pushed themselves out of their chrysalises and hung themselves from the ceiling of the netted cage, drying their drooping wings. We let the boys keep their "pets" inside the tent in our living room for a couple of days, but eventually we released them into our garden where, much to Noah's and Rowan's teary-eyed dismay, they fluttered over the picket fence and out of the yard, never to be seen again.

What I didn't know during the days we waited with high expectations for our chrysalises to metamorphose into butterflies in our living room is that long before monarch larvae hatch from their miniscule eggs, they already have everything they need within their DNA to become butterflies. According to scientists, the information for every part of the butterfly is stored in the caterpillar's cells, waiting to be unlocked.[1] When the caterpillar encases itself in the chrysalis, an enzyme begins the process of breaking down the physical tissue, in turn activating the imaginal cells I mentioned in the previous chapter, which ultimately form its new body parts.[2]

The key, though, is that these critical imaginal cells are not new; rather, they've been part of the caterpillar since the beginning, when it was merely a tiny egg clinging to the underside of leaf. In other words, the essence of the monarch butterfly was locked inside the caterpillar all along; it shed what it didn't need to become who it already was.

We love the metaphor of metamorphosis—caterpillar to chrysalis to butterfly—because we love the idea of rebirth. We all want the chance for a new beginning, a fresh start, a do-over. But the story of a monarch caterpillar's metamorphosis is perhaps less a story of rebirth and more a story of reemergence. A butterfly is not reborn as an utterly new insect; it simply reemerges as another version of itself.

"My identity does not begin when I begin to understand myself," Eugene Peterson writes in *Run with the Horses*. "There is something previous to what I think about myself, and it is what God thinks of me. That means that everything I think and feel is by nature a response, and the one to whom I respond is God. I never speak the first word. I never make the first move."[3] In other words, this spiritual journey we are on is not so much about being reborn into someone new, but about recognizing, receiving, and embracing who we already are, have always been and are meant to become.

Like the essence of the butterfly captured in the cells of the caterpillar, the essence of who we are—our true self— has already been born and is already created. We shed what we do not need to reveal what is already there. We receive what existed previous to our knowledge of ourselves. We receive what God gives us, what he has always been giving us, what has been there all along: our true self, the person God created us to become.

For most of my life I've searched for meaning and wholeness in all the wrong places. I thought I could find meaning by belonging to a certain group of people or by achieving particular successes. I thought I could manufacture wholeness by winding the vine of achievement and success tighter and tighter around and around myself. What I have discovered is that meaning isn't "out there"—it isn't something to be grasped at; it isn't somewhere I need to push my way into or conform to. Meaning and wholeness are in me, and they have been all along. As St. Francis reportedly said, "What we are looking for is what is looking."[4] In other words, we are searching for what we already have: our own selves.

"Looking within is often the last place we think of looking," says author and Jungian psychologist James Hollis. Instead, we ask, *How can I fix this? How can I work harder? How can I make this happen? How can I change the circumstances or contort myself to fit within those circumstances?* But those are not the best questions to ask, because meaning is not created externally. "Meaning is confirmed from the inside."[5]

This is why it's so important that we let ourselves feel and why it is so important to listen to and acknowledge what our bodies are telling us. The physical sensations we experience in our bodies are an avenue to our feelings, and our feelings are an avenue to our soul. Our soul will tell us who we are becoming. Our soul will confirm from the inside who we already are.

## There Will Always Be Vines

I wish I could tell you that the invasive vine is no longer wrapped around the pine tree in my neighbor's yard. I want to give you a storybook ending. I want to tell you that I walked by one day and was delighted to see that the vine had been stripped away, chopped up, and tossed into the compost pile. I want to tell you the pine tree is now growing again and thriving, with new branches and lush boughs and tender greening needles. I would love to give you that beautifully wrapped-up metaphor to complete this story.

Alas, I can't, because it's not true. These days I walk alone past the pine tree. Our sweet girl and my daily walking companion, Josie, died unexpectedly last fall, and honestly, months later, I am still aching from the loss of her. Every day when I walk alone past the pine tree in my neighbor's yard, I think about Josie, remembering how we always stopped there so she could sniff at the lawns and the leaves and the pine cones collecting at the side of the street. And every day when I walk past the pine tree alone, I see that the tree is still dying, still suffocating under the weight of the vine. The vine is more robust and vibrant than ever.

This, I realize, is not a perfect or a beautiful ending to this story, but it's a real one. The truth is, there are no perfect endings, at least here on earth. There will always be grief, suffering, heartbreak, and struggle. There will always be vines. There will always be parts of our lives that we will need to unwind and let go, pieces of ourselves that we no longer need and are being asked to release. We cling to some of these parts and pieces more tightly than others; sometimes it takes years to truly let go. Sometimes when we do manage to let go, we discover later that we missed the root and have to begin again.

This is why the seasons are a fitting metaphor for our journey. Fall, winter, spring, and summer cycle one into the next, month after month, year after year, decade after decade—always beginning again. And yet, the seasons do not simply repeat in the exact same way. Rather, there is growth and change, sometimes dramatic, more often subtle, along the way. Creation has a long arc, and each season offers something necessary for the next. Autumn's release opens the way to winter's rest. Winter's rest restores for spring's rejuvenation. Spring's rejuvenation blossoms into summer's abundance.

It is the same with the seasons of our soul. Our journey of transformation has a long arc. We are never finished with our changing during our time on earth, nor do we ever fully arrive while we are here. We simply circle closer. We release what we no longer need. We rest. We are sustained and renewed. We reap abundantly. And then we begin again, circling ever closer to becoming who we already are.

# Acknowledgments

Deepest thanks to Julie Davis for her stellar copyediting skills and generous support; to Eva Polakovičová for a beautiful cover illustration; Euan Monaghan for book design; and to Deidra Riggs, Kimberly Coyle, Trina Cress, Amber Pankonin, Patty Forsberg, the Kindred Collective, Lotus House of Yoga and the Thursday morning Contemplate Lincoln group for continual support, friendship, community, encouragement, and love.

Gratitude and love to Rowan, for always making it fun; to Noah, for helping me see; and to Brad, for asking the hard questions and walking along with me to uncover the answers.

# Notes

CHAPTER ONE: PINE TREE AND VINE

1  David Benner, *The Gift of Being Yourself: The Sacred Call to Self-Discovery* (Downers Grove, IL: InterVarsity, 2015), 88.

2  Thomas Merton, *New Seeds of Contemplation* (New York: New Directions, 1961), 35.

3  Benner, *The Gift of Being Yourself*, 95–96.

4  David Whyte, *Consolations: The Solace, Nourishment and Underlying Meaning of Everyday Words* (Langley, WA: Many Rivers Press, 2015), 237.

5  Merton, *New Seeds of Contemplation*, 16.


CHAPTER TWO: GINGKO AND PIN OAK

1  Robert Krulwich, "Why Leaves Really Fall Off Trees," *All Things Considered*, NPR, October 30, 2009. https://www.npr.org/templates/story/story.php?storyId=114288700.

2  Lori Gottlieb, *Maybe You Should Talk to Someone* (New York: Harper, 2019).

3  "Enmeshment," *Good Therapy* (blog), last updated November 3, 2016, https://www.goodtherapy.org/blog/psychpedia/enmeshment.


CHAPTER THREE: WEEPING RIVER BIRCH

1  Merton, *New Seeds of Contemplation*, 47.

2  "Wait—Before You Use Pruning Sealer on Trees," Davey, April 14, 2016, https://blog.davey.com/2016/04/wait-before-you-use-pruning-sealer-on-trees/.

3  Rick Kemery, "Sap Bleed OK after Spring Pruning," *The Journal Gazette*, April 22, 2017, https://www.journalgazette.net/features/home-garden/20170422/sap-bleed-ok-after-spring-pruning.

4  Bessel Van der Kolk, *The Body Keeps the Score: Brain, Mind and Body in the Healing of Trauma* (New York: Penguin Press, 2015), 95–96.

CHAPTER FOUR: COMPOST AND SOIL

1 Luci Shaw, *Water My Soul: Cultivating the Interior Life* (Vancouver, BC: Regent College Publishing, 2003), 61.

2 Shaw, *Water My Soul*, 62.

3 Julia Cameron, *The Artist's Way: A Spiritual Path to Higher Creativity*, 25th Anniversary Edition (New York: TarcherPerigee, 2016), 83.

4 Christine Valters Paintner, *The Soul of a Pilgrim: Eight Practices for the Journey Within* (Notre Dame, IN: Sorin Books, 2015), 101–102.

5 Parker Palmer, "Fierce with Reality: Living and Loving Well to the End," *On Being*, July 8, 2015, https://onbeing.org/blog/fierce-with-reality-living-and-loving-well-to-the-end/.

CHAPTER FIVE: ROSE BUSHES WRAPPED IN BURLAP

1 Christine Valters Paintner, *The Artist's Rule: Nurturing Your Creative Soul with Monastic Wisdom* (Notre Dame, IN: Soren Books, 2011), 52.

2 Paintner, *The Artist's Rule*, 51.

3 Katherine May, *Wintering: The Power of Rest and Retreat in Difficult Times* (New York: Riverhead Books, 2020), 3.

4 Scott Barry Kaufman, "The Quiet Ego," interview by Jocelyn K. Glei, *Hurry Slowly*, April 16, 2019, https://hurryslowly.co/scott-barry-kaufman/.

5 Akiko Busch, *How to Disappear: Notes on Invisibility in a Time of Transparency* (New York: Penguin Press, 2019), 9.

6 Busch, *How to Disappear*, 63.

7 Busch, 63.

8 Eugene Peterson, *Run with the Horses: The Quest for Life at Its Best* (Downers Grove, IL: InterVarsity, 2009), 141.

9 Whyte, *Consolations*, 113–114.

10 Cal Newport, *Digital Minimalism: Choosing a Focused Life in a Noisy World* (New York: Portfolio/Penguin, 2019), xx.

11 Newport, *Digital Minimalism*, 28.

### CHAPTER SIX: STELLA THE CAT

1 John O'Donohue, *Anam Cara: A Book of Celtic Wisdom* (New York: HarperCollins, 1997), 61–62.

2 O'Donohue, *Anam Cara*, 62.

3 O'Donohue, 59.

4 Colleen Walsh, "What the Nose Knows," *The Harvard Gazette*, February 27, 2020, https://news.harvard.edu/gazette/story/2020/02/how-scent-emotion-and-memory-are-intertwined-and-exploited/.

5 O'Donohue, 58.

6 Kathleen Norris, *The Cloister Walk* (New York: Riverhead Books, 1997), 11.

### CHAPTER SEVEN: GREENHOUSE PHILODENDRON

1 Jenny Odell, *How to Do Nothing: Resisting the Attention Economy* (Brooklyn: Melville House Publishing, 2019), 137.

2 Cameron, *The Artist's Way*, 183.

3 O'Donohue, *Anam Cara*, 57.

4 Cameron, 123.

5 Walt Whitman, "Song of Myself," poetryfoundation.org, accessed January 27, 2022, https://www.poetryfoundation.org/poems/45477/song-of-myself-1892-version.

### CHAPTER EIGHT: TULIP BULBS

1 Richard Rohr, *The Wisdom Pattern: Order—Disorder—Reorder* (Cincinnati: Franciscan Media, 2020), 121.

2 Rohr, *The Wisdom Pattern*, 121–132.

3 Ann Voskamp, *The Greatest Gift: Unwrapping the Full Love Story of Christmas* (Carol Stream, IL: Tyndale, 2013), 72.

4 O'Donohue, *Anam Cara*, 123.

5 Matthew Fox, *Julian of Norwich: Wisdom in a Time of Pandemic—and Beyond* (Bloomington, IN: iUniverse, 2020), 38.

CHAPTER NINE: SPRING PEEPERS AND MAPLE SAP

1  Wendell Berry, *The Unforeseen Wilderness: Kentucky's Red River Gorge* (Berkeley: Counterpoint, 2006), as quoted in Parker Palmer, "To Be at Peace with Our Essential Loneliness," *On Being*, May 7, 2017, https://onbeing.org/blog/parker-palmer-to-be-at-peace-with-our-essential-loneliness/.

2  Paintner, *The Artist's Rule*, 96.

3  Pierre Teilhard de Chardin, "Prayer of Teilhard de Chardin," Ignatianspirituality.com, accessed December 19, 2020, https://www.ignatianspirituality.com/prayer-of-theilhard-de-chardin/.


CHAPTER TEN: RED FOX IN THE WOODPILE

1  Karla McLaren, *The Language of Emotions: What Your Feelings Are Trying to Tell You* (Boulder, CO: Sounds True, 2010), 7.

2  McLaren, *The Language of Emotions*, 29 and 31.

3  May, *Wintering*, 236.

4  McLaren, *The Language of Emotions*, 295.

5  McLaren, 312.

6  Aundi Kolber, *Try Softer: A Fresh Approach to Move Us out of Anxiety, Stress, and Survival Mode—and into a Life of Connection and Joy* (Carol Stream, IL: Tyndale, 2020), 156.

7  Tom Seymour, "Everything You Need to Know about the Vagus Nerve," *Medical News Today*, June 28, 2017, https://www.medicalnewstoday.com/articles/318128 and Jill Seladi-Schulman, "Vagus Nerve Overview," *Healthline*, updated October 22, 2021, https://www.healthline.com/human-body-maps/vagus-nerve.

8  Deb Dana, "Befriending Your Nervous System," Interview by Tami Simon, *Insights at the Edge*, Sounds True, June 16, 2020, https://resources.soundstrue.com/podcast/deb-dana-befriending-your-nervous-system/.

9  Kolber, *Try Softer*, 171.

10 Dana, "Befriending Your Nervous System," https://resources.soundstrue.com/podcast/deb-dana-befriending-your-nervous-system/.

11 Kolber, 19.

CHAPTER ELEVEN: PRESCRIBED BURNS AND GREENING BOG

1   "Prescribed Burning of Prairies," Iowa State University, Natural
    Resource Ecology and Management, updated September 4, 1998,
    https://www.nrem.iastate.edu/class/assets/aecl535b/fire.htm and
    Tyson Seirer, "Smooth Brome Grass—Control in CRP Fields,"
    USDA Natural Resources Conservation Service of Kansas.
    https://www.nrcs.usda.gov/wps/portal/nrcs/detail/ks/newsroom/
    features/?cid=nrcs142p2_033533.

2   Matthew Fox, *Illuminations of Hildegard of Bingen* (Rochester,
    VT: Bear & Company, 2003), 43.

3   Fox, *Illuminations*, 44.

4   Fox, 44.

5   Matt Candeias, "The Incredible Feat of a Resurrection Plant,"
    *In Defense of Plants* (blog), November 28, 2017, http://www.
    indefenseofplants.com/blog/2017/11/27/the-incredible-feat-of-a-
    resurrection-plant.

CHAPTER TWELVE: THINNING ZINNIAS

1   Mary Oliver, "The Summer Day," Library of Congress, accessed
    January 29, 2022, https://www.loc.gov/programs/poetry-and-
    literature/poet-laureate/poet-laureate-projects/poetry-180/all-
    poems/item/poetry-180-133/the-summer-day/.

CHAPTER THIRTEEN: PRAYING MANTIS, MONARCH
BUTTERFLIES, AND MUSTARD SEEDS

1   "Abundance," Dictionary.com, https://www.dictionary.com/
    browse/abundance?s=t.

2   Thomas Keating, *Meditations of the Parables of Jesus* (Chestnut
    Ridge, NY: Crossroad, 2010), 10.

CHAPTER FOURTEEN: GERMAN HEIRLOOM
TOMATOES AND PUMPKIN VINES

1   Linda Pearce, "How Stanislas Wawrinka Failed at Becoming a
    Failure," *The Sydney Morning Herald*, January 23, 2014, https://
    www.smh.com.au/sport/tennis/how-stanislas-wawrinka-failed-
    at-becoming-a-failure-20140122-3195v.html.

2   Katrina Kenison, *Magical Journey: An Apprenticeship in
    Contentment* (New York: Grand Central Publishing, 2013), 173.

3   Augusto Cuginotti, "Imaginal Cells: The Caterpillar's Job to
    Resist the Butterfly," Augusto Cuginotti: Facilitating Context-
    sensitive Systems Change, accessed March 17, 2021, https://
    augustocuginotti.com/imaginal-cells-caterpillars-job-to-resist-
    butterfly/.


CHAPTER FIFTEEN: MINNESOTA CEDAR TREE

1   Keating, *Open Heart*, 7.

2   Keating, 65–66.

3   Sue Monk Kidd, *When the Heart Waits: Spiritual Direction for
    Life's Sacred Questions* (New York: HarperCollins, 1990), 136.

4   Keating, 81.

5   Rohr, *The Wisdom Pattern*, 135.

6   Rohr, 135.

7   Rohr, 140.

8   Rohr, 136.


EPILOGUE

1   "Ask Dr. Universe," University Communications Network,
    Washington State University, accessed November 19, 2020,
    https://askdruniverse.wsu.edu/2015/04/06/caterpillar-
    soup/#:~:text=During%20the%20first%20couple%20days,legs%20
    form%20inside%20the%20chrysalis.&text=Then%2C%20the%20
    chrysalis%20turns%20a%20very%20a%20dark%20color.

2   Anthony Bouchard, "Here's What Happens inside a Caterpillar's Chrysalis," Labroots, September 22, 2019, https://www.labroots.com/trending/plants-and-animals/15714/here-s-happens-inside-caterpillar-s-chrysalis.

3   Peterson, *Run with the Horses,* 39–40.

4   Geneen Roth, *This Messy, Magnificent Life: A Field Guide* (New York: Scribner, 2018), 41.

5   James Hollis, "The Goal of Life is Meaning, Not Happiness," interview by Tami Simon, *Insights at the Edge,* Sounds True, June 9, 2020, https://www.resources.soundstrue.com/podcast/james-hollisthe-goal-of-life-is-meaning-not-happiness/.

Made in United States
Orlando, FL
31 August 2022

21804125R10129